Resilience:
The Life-Saving
Skill of Story

The *Resilience* Series

Resilience: Adapt and Plan for the New Abnormal - in the COVID-19 Coronavirus Pandemic
Gleb Tsipursky

Resilience: Aging with Vision, Hope and Courage in a Time of Crisis
John C. Robinson

Resilience: Connecting with Nature in a Time of Crisis
Melanie Choukas-Bradley

Resilience: Going Within in a Time of Crisis
P. T. Mistlberger

Resilience: Grow Stronger in a Time of Crisis
Linda Ferguson

Resilience: Handling Anxiety in a Time of Crisis
George Hoffman

Resilience: Navigating Loss in a Time of Crisis
Jules De Vitto

Resilience: The Life-Saving Skill of Story
Michelle Auerbach

Resilience: Virtual Teams - Holding the Center When You Can't Meet Face-to-Face
Carlos Valdes Dapena

Resilience: Virtually Speaking - Communicating at a Distance
Tim Ward and Teresa Erickson

Resilience:
The Life-Saving
Skill of Story

Michelle Auerbach

CHANGEMAKERS
BOOKS

Winchester, UK
Washington, USA

JOHN HUNT PUBLISHING

First published by Changemakers Books, 2020
Changemakers Books is an imprint of John Hunt Publishing Ltd., No. 3 East Street,
Alresford, Hampshire SO24 9EE, UK
office@jhpbooks.com
www.johnhuntpublishing.com
www.changemakers-books.com

For distributor details and how to order please visit the 'Ordering' section on our website.

Text copyright: Michelle Auerbach 2020
Cover art: Anna Moore 'The Kintsugi Heart'

ISBN: 978 1 78904 701 1
978 1 78904 702 8 (ebook)
Library of Congress Control Number: 2020937098

A CIP catalogue record for this book is available from the British Library.

Design: Stuart Davies

UK: Printed and bound by CPI Group (UK) Ltd, Croydon, CR0 4YY
Printed in North America by CPI GPS partners

We operate a distinctive and ethical publishing philosophy in
all areas of our business, from our global network of authors to
production and worldwide distribution.

Contents

Foreword   1

Chapter 1 – Story Will Save Your Life   2

Chapter 2 – You Are Not A Red Rubber Ball   17

Chapter 3 – Everyday Heroes and Superheroes   37

Chapter 4 – Please Turn On The Light   56

Previous Titles

The Third Kind of Horse
ISBN: 978-0-9569525-4-7

Alice Modern
ISBN:978-1-880977-44-6

"We tell ourselves stories in order to live."
Joan Didion

Acknowledgements

A list can be a story of collaboration, community, creativity, and care. Thank you to the title crew: Julie Maxwell, Kim Dana Kupperman, and Nicole Civita, who are good where I am not. I would like to extend enormous gratitude to the people I interviewed for this book. Some people became back story, some were more visible, but all of you are my heroes: Catlyn Keenan, Nicole Civita, Meesha Brown, Reggie Hubbard, Carmen Cool, Rachel Goble, Tim Hurson, Tim Ward, Marc Hurwitz, Bhanu Kapil, Jessica Pfeiffer, Kelly Diels, Becky O'Brian, Isabel Foxen Duke, Leonardo Munoz, Cheryl Geffrion, Sheva Carr, Lisa Woolfork, Rash Trumble, Beth Slazak, Selassie Atadika, Ismet Mamoun, Tom Lombardo, Sheva Carr, Meg Bradbury, Nigel Slater, Becky O'Brian, Shanna Lewis, and Alexis Pauline Gumbs. As a zip file for acts of kindness– Desi del Valle, Ann Fleming, Melinda and Tom Wirsing, Diana Miller, Diana Witaschek, and Claire Shafe. Thanks to the people who make the magic happen for my story work: Solveig Ellingboe Nelson, Brooke McAnally, Carolyn Oakley, Paul Breaux, Marlene Lepkoski. Thank you Tim Ward, Publisher of Changemakers Press and John Hunt, owner and publishing manager of John Hunt Publishing for putting me in the way of great stories and sharing your joy in the written word. Thank you Joan Stein for so much editing. Kelly Diels, you make me cool. Safia Radha Ohlson, sine qua non. I am cooped up with the best family ever, even if all of you are not in the house – Zoe Auerbach, Emma Auerbach Brode, and Zach Brode – you always keep me human. Step-kids are a gift when I need distraction – Sam Cole, Chris Cole, and Ben Cole. Thank you Allan for being a storyteller in your own work, and for sharing in the redemptive power of story.

Foreword by the Publisher

"What can we do to help?"

In a time of crisis – such as the 2020 Covid-19 pandemic – we all have a natural impulse to help our neighbors. John Hunt, founder of John Hunt Publishing, asked this question of our company, and then offered a suggestion. He proposed producing a series of short books written by experts offering practical, emotional, and spiritual skills to help people survive in the midst of a crisis.

To reach people when they need it most, John wanted to accomplish this in forty days. Bear in mind, the normal process of bringing a book from concept to market takes at least eighteen months. As publisher of the JHP imprint Changemakers Books, I volunteered to execute this audacious plan. My imprint publishes books about personal and social transformation, and I already knew many authors with exactly the kinds of expertise we needed. That's how the *Resilience* series was born.

I was overwhelmed by my authors' responses. Ten of them immediately said yes and agreed to the impossible deadline. The book you hold in your hands is the result of this intensive, collaborative effort. On behalf of John, myself, the authors and production team, our intention for you is that you take to heart the skills and techniques offered to you in this these pages. Master them. Make yourself stronger. Share your newfound resilience with those around you. Together, we can not only survive, but learn how to thrive in tough times. By so doing, we can find our way to a better future.

Tim Ward
Publisher, Changemakers Books
May 1, 2020

Chapter 1

Story Will Save Your Life

All of our learning, our ability to change, our empathy and connection to other humans, and our ability to live a good life, comes from storytelling and listening. All of the skills we need to be resilient in a crisis we learn through story, and all the skills we have that we need to share with others we share through story. Story mediates our world and ourselves in ways that increase our adaptability and improve our world. It's not complicated. It already lives in our brains, bodies, and minds and we can access it through a little practice and some remembering of the skills we all had as children. Once we get fluent in storytelling and story listening, we are able to adapt, learn, teach, share, understand, and cope in ways that will allow us to move with change and lend a hand when the people around us are not moving. The process is available to all of us; it transforms us and our lives and can save the world.

I was on the phone this week with a group of hospital chaplains from across the United States. It is week two of sheltering at home here in Colorado, and the hospitals these chaplains serve are seeing many of the 65,000 COVID-19 cases we currently know about in the United States. They wink into existence on Zoom one at a time, the first being the chaplain to an Emergency Medicine group who are waiting for the flood of cases to sweep through their doors. Things are calm, but in the background I can hear the erratic noises of ER staff working, and occasionally someone comes into view behind the speaker, masked and gowned and gloved, looking determined as they pass through the frame. He initiates our group check-in, saying, "We have no PPE, and everyone is functioning in a state of heightened anxiety. Our spouses have lost jobs, our kids are at home and we don't know if we are infecting them, and there is a feeling of rage in everyone I talk to."

He has to explain to those of us who don't know hospital jargon that PPE is Personal Protective Equipment. They don't have the gloves and the masks and the gear they need to keep themselves safe. His face is serene but drawn, and his voice trembles inside his six-foot frame as he looks into the camera and asks us for something. "What can I do? I have no medical training. All I know how to do is to park myself on the unit and be a sounding board for their frustration. Let them tell me their stories."

Someone in the group asks him, "Does that help?"

His face changes, pink cheeks appear as he smiles, and we can all feel the relaxation through the Internet, "Yes, honestly, listening to them tell their stories de-escalates the frustration for them and for me."

The call continues. I'm lost thinking about that deceptively small moment of telling a story or hearing a story, and feeling better, connected, stronger, more human and alive. One of my favorite writers, who is also an amazing theologian and thinker, Madeline L'Engle, wrote: "Stories make us more alive, more human, more courageous, more loving." I know that to be true, even more now when we are so separated and yet so needy of connection. My fears and my anxiety creep up on me; this is common even without a global pandemic. What works most times is to immerse myself in story. I watch a show on Netflix, I pick up a book, I call a friend and ask them: "Tell me what's up with you." All of those story immersions allow me to move myself into another world, a different reality, and in so doing, change my mind, heart and life.

This is the very first skill of story, and you already have it. Story changes your mood, your feelings, your emotions, and your world. You may find it in a book, a show, or a conversation, but you already have the skill to shift your mood and your reality. It is a simple step but a big one: realize that you don't like where you are, that you feel prickly, depleted, uncomfortable, angry, anxious, or scared, and decide you'd like to feel a different way.

I have always been interested in the "how" of things. How do you do that, what do you do first, how does it work? We will have the How To section for every skill or tool we discuss and I will give you a practical way to use it right away, this very moment.

How To: Shifting Your Mood

Stories transport us to a new place and we can use them like an airline ticket or a bus pass. The first step is to know where you are. On any trip, like in any story, you start somewhere with a need to be somewhere else. Every character in every story experiences this. For us, we can check our feelings to find out if we need to move. Our feelings happen in our bodies. There is great research that shows cross-culturally, we all experience our feelings in similar ways and places in our bodies. So, fear hits us in the pit of our stomachs, joy in our heart, and anger in the shoulders or back of our arms. If we want to change our mood, we need to be aware we are somewhere we'd rather not be. Our body tells us.

In crises or under stress, a lot of the information coming from our bodies is going to let us know that we would rather not be where we are. Story is the intervention for discomfort, and the gateway to whatever other tools you have: meditation, movement, a good cry, a dance party in your living room, or Heartmath, which we will learn in Chapter 4. Once you have identified that you want to change where you are, lean on story. Pick up a book, start a conversation, listen to a podcast, or watch a movie. Or simply tell yourself the story that I was upset or mad or hurt or scared and I noticed, and then I decided to go for a run. It may sound strange, but research tells us that narrating life is a form of storytelling that gives us some distance from ourselves and helps us make better choices.

Eliciting Story

I've been talking to a lot of the people I know in other parts of the world to elicit stories and to transport myself somewhere else. In a Zoom conversation, I was transported to Milan, where my friend Matteo lives. He was sitting in his kitchen, surrounded by pots and pans and the detritus of cooking. He lifted up a cake, and showed my daughter and me, and our friend Marina who was in her living room in Trieste, through the screen. "Look, I put a banana in it and it was— " Here he kisses his fingers in true Italian style. "I have been cooking for hours every day. It's been six weeks. I am already a very good cook."

There are questions you can ask that will lead to a good story, and that can make anyone a great storytelling. One of them is as simple as saying "So, what's going on?" That is what I asked Matteo.

"Everything here is different; it is so simple, and we are all very careful with each other. My grocer, where I buy my vegetables, we talk every day. He tells me what's happening on his street, I tell him about mine. Then I order, and leave him money downstairs. He brings the vegetables and waves at me from the window. I love my grocer. He keeps me fed and happy and so, life, it goes on."

Matteo's story brings me to his neighborhood in Milan, where I have never been, but I can feel his empty street, the grocer bringing the vegetables for Matteo's cooking extravaganza, and the distance from the front door where the grocer leaves the vegetables and the sixth-floor apartment where Matteo cooks them and the rickety tiny elevator in between that Matteo says scares him every time he steps in. "I don't take the elevator at all," Marina chimes in, "and I live on the sixth floor." She makes a muscle with her arm and we all laugh. I am there, and I feel better just knowing what it feels like to be them, there, at this time in history, complete with banana cake and lots of stairs. Matteo's reality is a time machine and I know we will all be okay.

How To: Story Questions

The questions that elicit story from people are open ended questions. They cannot be answered yes or no, and they have no agenda. Some formulations include:

"What's going on?"
"Tell me what happened?"
"What did you do about that?"
"Then what happened next?"
"What do you want to have happen?"
"What are you doing right now?"
"What did you learn from that?"

Story Corps, an organization that records stories and shares them for posterity has a list of great story questions for all situations from parenting to military service. I've noticed that their questions have a simple equation. One that works with what I know about the plots of great stories. Theirs says, have you ever + what was it like + what did you learn = great story. So, "Have you ever been to another country? What was it like there? What did you learn from that trip?" And then, let the person talk.

What is Story?

This brings up the question: What is a story? For our uses, I am going to give you a very pragmatic and functional definition.

Story is a narrative in which we tell about our own experiences, external events, memories (ours or otherwise), or history that we lived or someone else lived. Stories can be shared by talking, reading, watching and seeing, listening, and many other modes. Stories exist however we as humans share our experiences with ourselves, other people, groups, communities, and the world. Story is a way humans create meaning in our worlds, interpret what happens to us, and make sense of our shared experiences.

To create stories with resonance, stories that reach people emotionally, and that have the capacity to elicit all the science and magic possible, we use an age-old process that is called the Arc of Narrative. For us, as we work on the life-saving skills of story, we can boil that down to a story equation you could write on the back of your hand.

What's Going On + What I Did About It + What Happened = Story

This can fit all sorts of stories – a trip, something I learned, a catastrophe that befell me, or something from my childhood. The same three-part structure will transport people, help them learn, and even pass on some data if you need to. What it does, because it follows the classical structure of a plot from any great book or movie, is help us become transported from where we are to somewhere else. Tim Ward, who teaches people how to give successful TED talks says, "The formula for every story is: problem, action, result."

How To: Story Equation

Write it on a sticky note and post it somewhere you can see it:

What's Going On + What I Did About It + What Happened = Story

When we are concerned about saving lives, it's important to have an idea of what stories can do, what to expect of them, and how they work to create resilience. Meesha Brown, President of PCI Media, educator and changemaker and story learning advocate, explains how her organization looks at what story can do.

Meesha settles into her chair in New York City, and gives

me the lowdown. "In our field of humans learning through communication, we have three ways to measure the efficacy of a story. First there is a thing called KAP. KAP stands for Knowledge, Attitude, and Practice change. I think that is the *least* stories should do. We are also equally interested in these other two things: community and connection. Have we told the story and facilitated conversation around the story in such a way that the connections between people and organizations and entities and communities are stronger? If we do that, we are successful. We want the connection that exists from the story to take on the next challenge or to continue the work of taking on this challenge, even when we are not there.

"So, let me give you this wonderful, amazing example of the community piece that I love. Eighteen months ago, I went to La Paz, Bolivia for the first time to visit our team there. Sometime around 2012, we had a program sponsored by the United States State Department on human trafficking. As part of the methodology, we created a story called *Caldera*, the Cauldron, a radio drama, basically a novella. We always work with local radio stations as much as possible because radio is a great place for dialogue. In this iteration of the implementation, we worked with youth groups that learned how to be the radio hosts and facilitate calling conversation with special guests, experts, police officers, some teachers, some youth, to have this informed conversation around the stuff that was happening in the drama as a mirror for life. By 2014, the funding had run out on the programs and I thought we were done. I go to visit, eighteen months ago in 2018, and Johnny, our country director says, 'I want to take you up to El Alto, the mountain city right above La Paz, because there are some people I want you to meet.'

"We walk into this tiny little community radio station and there are fifteen young women, ages twelve to nineteen, sitting in a circle. What I found out was that they have been hosting their own radio show since the program ended when our funding ran out." She was awed that those young women owned the conversation and kept it going all those years.

The final thing story does is create capacity. Successful stories allow people to learn things about themselves that have always been true, but they didn't realize. Story is a beautiful magical technology that brings forth the really good things that already exist in us and in one another." Meesha smiled when she explained this to me, looking like a Good Fairy who has story as a magic wand that she gives to communities to bring out the best of who we are as individuals, communities, and even humanity.

In order to get to any of the outcomes Meesha described, we need to be able to inhabit a larger view than what's in our own heads. Dr. Mark Hurwitz, a Canadian neuroscientist you will meet in Chapter 2, introduced me to a term and a concept for how that works. He called it "transportability". Transportability describes our ability to inhabit a story, to move out of our own minds and into the minds of others. This skill we all innately have allows us to use story to learn, change behaviors and attitudes, and make connection. We are able to leave our own minds and join others in theirs or invite them into ours. Being in Matteo's mind, six weeks into extreme social distancing, allowed me to feel better about my future. It made Matteo, as the storyteller, feel less alone. I was in his head with him there for a second. When we got off the phone, he said, "Thank you for coming to Milano for cocktails." And raised his glass. I did not get to share the Italian red that shimmered in the crystal, but I was in every other way, really there.

The three-part story equation will lead your listener to emotional connection, care, and enjoyment of your story, so rest assured you can bring someone there. It also works when the other person is a book or a movie. Some readers, according to research, still hear the voices of fictional characters when they put a book down or step out of a movie, kind of like being possessed by story. Some people even report that the characters changed the decisions they would make or the way they think, feel, and live. So, this three-part equation can teach, it can transport, it can help us change our mood, and it can help us to change people's minds and give them the information they need to make decisions.

The understanding that we learn from another person's stories is age old. The Greek philosopher Aristotle first talked about what he called "catharsis" in his *Poetics* somewhere between 384-322 B.C.E. His theory was that we can watch a play (or read a book or listen to a story) and we are transported into the story. We experience what the characters experience, and we go through everything with them. We learn from the mistakes and the decisions the characters make in the stories in much the same way we would learn from our own, except that we are safely in the audience and don't need to actually do the dangerous or risky thing ourselves. At the end, we feel better, and we are better, because of what we heard or watched or saw. We are transported to another place, time, story, or experience and we come back different.

Sharing What Matters Through Story

It is powerful for a storyteller when someone listens to you and you can feel they are right there with you. That's what worked for the Emergency Department chaplain when he was able to just listen to the staff. He could affirm for them that this is real, this is happening, and this is important, your experience is important to me as well as to you. I was there with you, you brought me along. For the listener, this shift in perception gives us a new perspective. For the teller, it is a way to crystalize our lives in front of us, visibly. That perspective reflects back to us our reality, too, and we are able to be human and learn from each other. This capacity can change our thinking, but it also changes our behavior.

We don't need to live an extraordinary life to have good

stories. In fact, we just need to tell the ordinary things with the story equation and we can create magic. Pay attention to what you find compelling, funny, riveting, or heart-warming. We can use those things to tell the best stories, the ones with the most emotion and connection, because they are ours.

My grandfather was a dentist, part of an immigrant family, and a curmudgeon. He told his grandkids stories all day about different experiences he had, from hanging wallpaper to being an Army dentist in World War II. One of his most famous stories was about a certain high-ranking officer who always wanted to jump the line and use his privilege to make people do what he wanted. One day, this officer came to the office where my grandfather was working on an enlisted man. He was in the middle of filling a cavity when the officer swept the door open, stormed in, and said, "Dr. Gordon, I need you to fix this tooth." My grandfather, who did not believe in the use of Novocain, and had some poor guy's mouth propped open with a drill, didn't even turn around. The officer said, "I have rank here, and I am ordering you to stop what you are doing and work on my tooth." Again, my grandfather did not turn around or even slow down his drilling. "I am ordering you!" The officer had reached his limit. Well, so had my grandfather and he finally replied, without turning around, "Teeth don't have rank, sir." The officer left in a huff and my grandfather finished with the guy who was getting the filling. He later sought out the officer and said, "I can see you now."

My grandfather managed to teach all his grandkids a lot through that one story. We learned what life was like in the military, what rank meant, what proper behavior was. We also learned how my grandfather felt about privilege, what he wanted us to do when we were asked to do something we thought was unethical, and even how to then continue to behave correctly by keeping our agreements with people. He never gave us a lecture about any of it, and yet, when I asked my cousin and my brother a few years ago, we all still remembered the story decades later, and we all felt the same way: it taught us about what our family's morals were, how to behave, what the 1940s were like in the Army, what was expected of us, and even how humans can correct injustice.

How To: Sharing Information Through Story

We can inform through story. We can even change behavior. We need to construct a good story with three parts – What's Going On + What I Did About It + What Happened, and people will remember it. I've seen this simple elegant equation used to convey information about how to combat climate change, how to lead in organizations, and even how to make a great dinner party when your first course is a disaster. I have seen it used to persuade the FDA, the CEOs of Fortune 50 companies, and middle school students. The writer Maya Angelou said, "At the end of the day people won't remember what you said or did, they will remember how you made them feel." All the research backs this up, and we will get into why in the next chapter.

Back in graduate school, I was in a mess of a relationship. My partner at the time was running a failing business, living in fear and anger, and needed me to prop up life in ways that left me exhausted, sad, and frankly scared. In the evenings I made chocolate chip cookies as a peace offering and then hid in my office to make it through the rough hours when we were both home. One weekend, I picked up a book a friend lent me, *The Crimson Petal and the White* by Michel Faber. All I wanted to do was take myself out of the current situation for a while to help me feel safe and calm. The story was so detailed and gorgeous that it worked. I was in Victorian England. However, the plot revolves around Sugar, a cunning and canny prostitute who props up the life of the man she is with. Sugar is treated poorly by William, who has purchased her from her Madam. She experiences real deprivation, abuse, unfairness, and danger.

I read that book under a ratty quilt, with endless cups of Earl Grey tea with sugar and cream. Huddled by the lamp I digested the book in gulps. It was so compelling to me because it spoke to me about my own life, but in reflection, it was safe because it was at a distance; it was not real, it was "just a story".

Reading the book on the couch, alone in the house, three things happened that we have discussed. The first was that I calmed down and was transported. The second was that I learned from the story because it created that equation – what her life was like + what she did about it + what happened. And then, I was able to apply it to my own life and make a decision.

Sugar's life radically affirmed for me that what was happening in my world was not okay. I felt how deeply Sugar was misused, abused, and harmed and I felt my ire rising. No one should be treated that way. I could see and hear and feel things in Michel Faber's story that I refused to see and hear and feel in my own life. I was transported. Once I'd been there, I could not go back to the life I was leading. I stood up from that couch, determined to save Sugar by saving myself. I could hear her in my head, whispering to me that she did not want me to experience her end, abused, cast out, and despondent. I ended the relationship and was gone from that house the next day. When friends would ask me "What made you do it after you ignored my advice?" I said, "A Victorian prostitute made me do it."

It was funny, and a good line. It had the benefit of also being true. I gained the same from Matteo in Italy, and on that call with the chaplains I could hear and see the same working on them. Seeing your, or someone else's, reality is a potent force for good. When people tell you what they did, it gives you options and ideas. When we tell what happened because of it, we tell our truths and our interpretations and make meaning with each other. Sharing our feelings and the stories that brought them about is powerful medicine for what ails us.

One of the administrators on the call recommended an article to the group to read and ponder. The article described the post-traumatic impacts of the SARS epidemic on hospital staff that had to manage the brunt of the cases in the United States. Those health care workers were still, two years out, experiencing signs of PTSD. She also sent us a Journal of the American Medical Association study on mental health in 1257 Chinese health care workers treating COVID-19 cases. The outcomes in both cases are what you would expect: anxiety, depression, insomnia, and distress. People carrying with them the stories and the pain that they have seen, the injury and the trauma.

Trauma and Story

Trauma is a fact of human life. We can't avoid it. While it is not evenly distributed in our culture, some people experience more based on race, religion, sexual orientation, economic access, body size, gender, gender expression, and other factors, it is still a reality no one can avoid. Even the most privileged people cannot construct a life free of trauma. It reminds me of a horror movie I saw in the 1980s in which this rich man had a phobia of bugs. He created a clean room in which he lived, where every precaution was taken, every item brought in was decontaminated, every person checked and re-checked. He thought he had manipulated nature to make a bug-free zone. He felt morally righteous. Does this sound familiar to our world right now? In the last scene of the movie, he pulls back the covers to climb in bed, and under the covers is a bed sized mass of crawling, seething cockroaches. He screams and the movie ends. Living in cheap student housing in New York City at the time, I remember feeling as though this was pretty accurate. You can only fight nature so far, and there simply will always be bugs. We are all living in a world right now where the bugs are everywhere.

A traumatic event is one in which a person or persons perceives themselves or others as threatened by an external force that seeks to annihilate them, and against which they are unable to resist and which overwhelms their capacity to cope. This is a paraphrase of the work of Dr. Bessel van der Kolk and Dr. Judith Herman. Maybe the oldest definition of trauma, and the most useful for us in this journey into storytelling as an intervention and a saving grace, comes from Johannes Hoffer, a medical student in Basel in 1688. Johannes Hofer wrote about patients who had mental sickness caused by a violent event and said it is a "…disease that is due essentially to a disordered imagination, whereby the part of the brain chiefly affected is that part in which the images are located."

So, if our imagination can become disordered, and our images and stories affected by events, then it is possible that by engaging our imaginations and our stories we can also heal and care for each other and ourselves. This is another benefit to story. It creates resilience to trauma by allowing us to feel safe, then teaching us what we need to learn, all while affirming the importance of our reality and leaving us better off. Story is a radical affirmation of possibility in times of crisis.

As we pondered those health care worker outcomes, Sheva Carr, who you will meet in Chapter 4, who was leading the call said, "Can we ride this wave? Get ahead of it? Learn from those studies and provide to each other, in the healthcare world or the general population, what we need to be resilient?"

I think we can, and I think we can do this for each other in all the places where life is stressful, traumatic, difficult, volatile, uncertain, and scary. We have all the tools we need, and they live in the stories we tell.

On the call, we ended with one of the chaplains, who was originally a nurse, interjecting a story about a doctor who works in her hospital. The doctor went shopping after pulling a double shift one day this week. She was exhausted, scared, and worried about her family as she pushed her cart around the store, blindly looking for food. Someone saw her in her scrubs and yelled at her "You are endangering us all by being here. Get out!" The doctor shrank into her dark world and started to leave the store. A shopper, who saw the whole thing asked for her grocery list. "Why don't you wait in the car and I'll bring you your food." The nurse told us that this story was shared on social media and it took fire in their town. People set up a system where average folks can shop for healthcare workers and bring them groceries so that they can care for their patients and their families, and the community can feel they are helping the people most impacted.

The hair stood up on the back of my neck. I had that feeling when someone just said a truth, deeper than I could articulate. That feeling also happens when the stories I hear break me out of my fear and small world and bring me into possibility. It always gives me the chills. I feel something like awe in those moments, and the enormity of who we can be. Story ignites in a community the passion to care, the possibility that we can belong more fully to each other, even when we are very far apart, even when we are so scared we can barely think. It gives us agency and power as individuals to be part of our world in ways we can only imagine.

Long Story Short

In this chapter there are techniques you can put to use right away. To go back to them, just look for the heading *How To:* and then the title. Sometimes you want a novel, the long winding journey, and sometimes you just want the *How To:* and that's this list.

There are also people mentioned who you might want to know more about. At the end of the book there is a Resources section where you can find all the people I interviewed and how to get more information about them.

How To: Shifting Your Mood
How To: Story Questions
How To: Story Equation
How To: Sharing Information Through Story

Chapter 2

You Are Not A Red Rubber Ball

Standing on the front steps of a fairy tale castle outside Santiago, Chile, Ana Elisa Anselmo asks us to break the perfect, white, porcelain bowls we are cradling in our hands. She is a small woman, with a slight smile in her clear eyes. She's speaking softly in the wide expanse of the steps and we all lean in to hear her. "Go ahead, break them, it will be okay," she says. We gently put the bowls into paper bags, and then let them drop onto the concrete. In the bright January sun, the shards in the bag look harsh, sharp and dangerous. We all troop back inside the castle holding our bags of brokenness. Laying out the shards on the table, Anselmo, an Art Restoration expert who works on fine art, and more recently on buildings that were destroyed by Chile's frequent earthquakes, keeps speaking softly about her work.

"We never try to make buildings look as though nothing happened," she tells us through her translator Diego, a poet and psychology student, and I can hear in his voice that he is moved by the conversation. "We want the building to be strong and broken at the same time. We want it to remind us that something happened, while being stronger than it was."

We stare at our shards and contemplate putting them back together. It will never be the same bowl, it can't possibly go back together, but it will be the old bowl, plus. The plus is hard to imagine with 30 pieces of porcelain in front of me on the table and no skill at art restoration. Ana says something I have heard before, "It will be strong in the broken places. But," she adds, "It will be even more beautiful because we valued it enough to save, to work on, and to make new. That is why we use gold to mend it. We want the brokenness to be beautiful."

We work for two hours with glue and gold paint, creating

bowls that look completely different than when we started. Mine has some parts that became dust, so it will never go back together again. I feel pressure and sadness in my chest as I work. It seems of the utmost importance that what I create be perfect, which is totally not possible. Ana and Diego appear behind my chair, and I am concentrating so hard in my frustration that I don't notice them.

"It will not be perfect," Ana says. Diego doesn't bother to translate. He just puts his hand on my shoulder and squeezes. "But it will be beautiful and strong."

Resilience

How we define resilience makes a difference in the stories we tell and the outcomes we look for when we are in crisis. Defining our outcomes is our prerogative as storytellers and we can set out to do it with clarity and purpose. The outcome Ana Elisa Anselmo gave me of resilience is my new definition. Not the same, but stronger, more beautiful, and well cared for.

Speaking to Tim Hurson, a speaker, writer and creativity theorist, we get on the subject of resilience. Tim gives the analogy that we think resilience will be like a red rubber ball. When you throw it, it hits the ground and comes back looking exactly the same as when you let it go. The ball is not damaged by the contact with the ground or the bounce. "This is not a good working definition of resilience. We don't come out of resilience experiences the same as when we went in." We are changed, even damaged, like those bowls. "We are different," Tim says, "But that might be a good thing."

How To: Point of View

We have the opportunity, when we tell stories or listen to stories, to tell people what is important to us, to share in creating the definition of resilience that speaks to our lives and our needs and their lives and their needs. You do have an opinion, and that opinion is called your Point of View. It percolates through all the stories you tell and the ones you find out there in the world that attract your attention. As you become versed in listening and telling stories, your Point of View will become clearer. You may only ever be able to explain it with a story, but it's there, and you have it, and we can all feel it when we listen to you. Defining your Point of View through story helps you manage and organize feelings and experiences and it is a natural outgrowth of thinking about and participating in story.

Think about all the stories you love, and think about whether there is a theme or an idea or a feeling running through them that stands out to you. That is a good test of your Point of View.

Lisa Woolfork is in the business of re-defining what resilience looks like in practice. She is an Associate Professor of English at the University of Virginia. She also created Black Women Stitch, a sewing group where Black lives matter. Lisa is the host and producer of the *Stitch Please* podcast, which is Black women, girls and femmes sewing. Lisa has such clarity of Point of View that you only need to listen to her once to understand that she knows where her stories are going and owns the outcomes. Lisa, deeply pondering what resilience means in her work said "Resilience and trauma go together. If we look back at our past, we can see guideposts that can help us to lead to a brighter future. It just requires a recalibration of vision. Sometimes it takes trauma to get to resilience and the future. It did in my case. One of the reasons I created Black Women Stitch was because of the cumulative effects of white supremacy and how it showed up in my sewing life and my sewing world. But it wasn't until there was a spark that I could make a change, be resilient."

She spent almost 20 years sewing with groups where she felt like she could never entirely be herself. Groups where white women made racist comments and Woolfork ignored them. "I could never be my fully entire self, and I knew this role I was playing was a portion of who I was but it wasn't all of who I was.

I knew I should go out and create a sewing space where I felt okay, but I did not have the motivation to do it."

She shakes her head and looks right at me through the camera on her computer to mine and her body settles. "It wasn't until after my experience with the deadly car attack in Charlottesville that things changed for me. My husband and I were counter-protesting and when the car came through, we were standing right there. It was just chaotic and traumatic on all these levels. When I tried to talk about it in my sewing circles, the White women who knew me, knew that I had been involved, wanted to shut down the conversation. It was hard to miss, as I had been doing media work, I'd been doing interviews, I'd been on the radio, I'd been on TV and in magazines. I'd been talking about this experience and about what it meant to fight and resist Nazis and white supremacist in one's own community. They just wanted nothing to do with it. They didn't understand why I would be bothered at all with it. They just wanted to shut down the conversation. It was a really terrible experience."

The trauma and the pain led her to create a place where she could be her full self and could support other Black women, girls, and femmes in being their full selves, too. She didn't immediately feel like organizing her own sewing community. But, when her husband said, "I don't think you are going to find a group of people who are Black Lives Matter activists in the sewing world," she was galvanized into action. She created Black Women Stitch, and while the people that are in Black Women Stitch are not mostly activists, they create a space where they can be their full selves and where the baseline is a shared belief in how deeply their lives do matter.

From that experience, Lisa Woolfork discovered that there was a long history of Black women sewing and even a museum in Kansas City devoted to Black women quilting. In defining her Point of View, Lisa Woolfork joined a history of cultural resilience and story.

When we define for ourselves what resilience means, and what the outcomes are that we most want to see, our stories become sharper, clearer, more powerful, and more poignant to the people who hear us. We can also surround ourselves with the stories that matter to us, and let those stories help define our world. They become a clear and powerful Point of View.

We all know from watching movies and reading books and listening to our friends and family that no hero of any story ever comes out the other end untouched by what they experienced. We also know that the deck is usually stacked against them. We see them fail, get beaten up by the antagonist, or stuck in a natural disaster, or lose something important to them. We like them all the more because of this. Stories need trouble in order to succeed. In research on how storytelling impacts our brains, this is called building empathy for the character. Oddly, success does not make us feel all warm and fuzzy towards another person in a story or in real life. Failure, risk, threat, and being in trouble are what make us care about each other. In our story equation this is the What Happened part. Something has to happen to engage our concern for the hero, and when you construct stories, remember that trouble makes us care.

Empathy

Research into empathy and storytelling tells us that two things happen in our brains when we are creating and listening to stories. One is we need to pay attention. Our world is full of distractions, exciting information, bright shiny objects, grocery lists, fears, thoughts, ideas and feelings. Our brain wants to jump on to the next thing, and the next. We have to do something to capture attention and hold onto it. If you imagine attention is like a flashlight your brain uses to see what's next, it can only really shine on one thing at a time. You can't be making a grocery list and then watching a movie at the same time. You may think you can, but it is simply not true. That is where the danger and the trouble come in. We are here to stay alive, to avoid danger, and to keep ourselves out of harm's way. Trouble gets our attention. When you tell a story and there is danger, your listeners focus. They want to learn a few things about What Happened and What Did You Do About It that will prevent them from being harmed. Thus you keep their attention. This is called emotional salience in the research, and it both allows you to focus and it helps us remember what we saw or heard or said.

The other thing that happens is empathy. We care about you, or the hero of the story you tell, and we want to see you and them make it. Paul Zak, in his research on story and empathy describes it this way: "Emotional simulation is the foundation for empathy and is particularly powerful for social creatures like humans because it allows us to rapidly forecast if people around us are angry or kind, dangerous or safe, friend or foe.

Such a neural mechanism keeps us safe, but also allows us to rapidly form relationships with a wider set of members of our species than any other animal does. The ability to quickly form relationships allows humans to engage in the kinds of large-scale cooperation that builds massive bridges and sends humans into space. By knowing someone's story—where they came from, what they do, and who you might know in common— relationships with strangers are formed."

Zak has done research on oxytocin in our brains, and says this is the neurochemical responsible for both empathy and transportability. "My lab pioneered the behavioral study of oxytocin and has proven that when the brain synthesizes oxytocin, people are more trustworthy, generous, charitable, and compassionate. I have dubbed oxytocin the "moral molecule" and others call it the love hormone. What we know is that oxytocin makes us more sensitive to social cues around us. In many situations, social cues motivate us to engage to help others, particularly if the other person seems to need our help."

How To: Create Empathy

To create empathy and to encourage people to be more compassionate and caring, all you need to do is use story. It acts as a transportation device to bring people out of their own small world and into a larger one where taking care of each other is the norm, and where pro-social behavior is more likely. Story is a skill, and one that will serve you well if you want to know more about the world and how to survive and thrive in it.

Story Listening

Listening is also a skill, and the other side of the storytelling coin. I asked an expert to share her understanding about listening and how to do it well. Carmen Cool is a therapist who works to help people heal their relationship with food and their bodies. She bridges therapy and activism, wanting to transform the field of psychotherapy so that it doesn't become another agent of oppression in people's lives. Carmen is the best listener I know, and when you sit across from her and talk, you can feel what you say reverberate in her. "How do you do it?" I asked her, as I was basking in the sun on my porch, computer balanced on my lap. "Give us some advice for being better listeners."

Carmen smiled at me and looked away for a second before she straightened her shoulders and said, "Pay attention to your body as you are listening. Things register in our bodies before they can register in our in our minds. So don't leave your body out of the process."

This resonates with the idea that our emotions are happening in our bodies when we tell the story, and when we are transported into someone else's stories we would feel it in the same place. I nodded and Carmen added a few other tips.

"It's much more of a generous listening to ask ourselves, 'What do I find myself curious about?' That will lead you deeper into someone's story. To be better listeners, we can bring our whole selves to the story and let ourselves be deeply curious about someone else's experiences."

This all made sense to me, but I wanted her to tell me how it works, how she is so good at it. I am the *How* person, so I want to know, "How do I do that?"

"I can give an example. If I'm listening to somebody and I notice that my jaw tightens, that's a clue for me about something I'm responding to in somebody else. If I let that be a source of curiosity and wisdom, I might slow down right there. I can say I want to hear more or tell me more about that. That means I am using my body as a cue to issue an invitation to the person to tell me a little bit more. Then, we are in it together."

How To: Listening

In the same way we feel our own emotions in our bodies, we can use our bodies as listening devices for other people's stories. Tune in like a radio, and listen for when music emerges from the static. Your body will tell you what's important, emotionally salient, what creates empathy and gets you involved. You can use that information, ask questions, elicit more story. Carmen Cool says that the magic invitation for listeners is "Tell me more." When you get a clear signal from your body, just ask the person: "Tell me more about that."

Story and Your Brain

Dr. Marc Hurwitz was walking around the conference center with his head shaved and his brain drawn on his skin in full color with what I hoped was not permanent marker. I followed him through the line to get lunch, staring at his moving 2D depiction of anatomy and wondered several things. "Who is this guy?" being the first obvious question. "What's that all about?" being the second, and "How do I learn more about this?" It turns out he is a neuroscientist and professor of Entrepreneurship at the University of Waterloo, and he was advertising his session at the conference debunking some myths about how we understand our brains and helping us think about cognition better. Of course, I went. As someone who has a "How to" mentality and also a deep love for the stories that show up in science, I was prepared to get comfortable. That's not what happened. Marc Hurwitz surprised a room full of expectant learners, notebooks out, ready to go, by telling us that much of what we think we know about the brain from popular reporting is what he calls "neuroporn." His definition of neuroporn goes something like this:

"I know it when I see it because it violates my sense of integrity. Generally, it shows up in three ways. First of all, it's the misuse of neuroscientific information by people who just aren't able to read the scientific papers. So they'll read something, and they'll read it uncritically, and not understand or take it out of context or not be able to interpret the information properly. The second is, there's a whole raft out there of just wrong information about neuroscience, myths like we only use 10% of our brain, or the whole we are either left brained or right brained idea. That's a classification of things that's just wrong. The third is that people use neuroscience information to bolster or justify a social science type of experiment. There's a famous and somewhat humorous study which shows that if you just add some neuroscience words to whatever you say, people are more likely to believe it, even if the neuroscience is rubbish."

For years I was storing up information about neuroscience and story in order to give some credibility to what I felt was true. I stood in rooms full of listeners and told them all sorts of things about mirror neurons and entrainment and amygdalae. In fact, I once gave a talk to 1000 entrepreneurs at Start Up Week that was all about the science of story, and felt so good about myself when I looked out over that sea of people and thought, "Now I have converted them." I was guilty of neuroporn. In the fluorescent lit room, the conversation went on. I took a little trip into shame and discomfort. When I finally came up for air, Hurwitz was in his element, telling us how to use what we do know about our brains to work and think better. A lot of what he said is pertinent to how to survive and thrive in crisis.

Marc Hurwitz gives the following advice to keep your brain working optimally: sleep, eat, exercise, and learn complex new skills.

I asked him if storytelling was a complex new skill and, after a brief discussion of what storytelling entails, he said yes. Usually those complex skills are things like learning a new language.

Marc explained that we're using 100% of our brain all the time, plus or minus 2% or 3% at the most. It's not true that you can magically up your brain capacity. In terms of space constraints, if you develop expertise in one thing, there's a possibility that it has an opposite effect on something else, simply because if you take up more of the brain to do one thing, then it might not function as well in another respect. Let me give you an example: the London cabbies who learned "The Knowledge", which is the 300 or 400 standard ways to navigate through London on the most popular routes. Learning this takes up a ton of the space in the hippocampus used for spatial memory. They become much worse at learning other new places. They're brilliant at London, and not so good navigating other places. Now, that may or may not apply to everything because, of course, the other thing you can do is create new connections between different neurons and complexify the brain and make it more intelligent.

Secondly, let's talk about the way people are resilient. One of the reasons we're resilient, according to Mark, is because we have schemas in our brain of the way the world works, and the longer we live in the world, the more often we see positive examples of those schemas working. When we see them working, it is more likely that those become fixed and resilient, because evidence to the contrary will no longer change those schemas or not change them very much.

From a storytelling perspective, one of the challenges we face in the modern day is the overabundance of ability to find stories which reinforce our existing schemas of the world. The main way of breaking through those schemas is by learning things that have emotional salience. Facts can only change our brain in very, very, small amounts and over a long period of time. We're actually quite resilient against facts if they contradict what we already think. However, if you can attach emotion to facts, which is what stories do, then you can overcome those barriers much more quickly.

Also, if you want people to engage their decision making (when you use story to persuade) you want them to be well rested, well fed, not have a lot of things competing for their attention, and you want them to have some skills at what they are doing. Marc did not say this, but from what he said, I want to add: pick your moment to tell a story very carefully. There are times when people will be able to engage with you, and times when no matter how carefully crafted or emotionally appealing your story is, the other person is just not ready.

Finally, the Brain Body Loop is critical. We need emotions to make decisions. As we have discussed, emotions live in the body, so our brains and bodies need to work together.

He shared a few other important ideas, but his final mention was "stay away from neuroporn."

I called Marc Hurwitz a few months later, feeling stung about my neuroporn past, and asked him to talk about this concept of what we know about our brains and what is either speculation or flat out misuse of information. I needed to get clear. I was sitting in my car, parked on a leafy street outside a store I needed to go into, but I pushed the seat back, balanced my phone on the steering wheel and gave him my full attention while he gave me some do's and don'ts.

How To: **Work With Your Brain**

You are already using 100% of your brain, so give yourself a break.

Facts don't change our schemas, feelings do – lean into the feelings and the story.

If you want people to be good decision makers, let them sleep, feed them, and give them decisions that they actually know something about.

We need emotions to make decisions, so don't fall into the trap that it all happens in your brain. Decisions happen in your body too.

"So, how do we explain everything we know about story if we can't use all the things about neurotransmitters and brain anatomy?" I asked.

"Oh, that," he said, "we know it works. Storytelling does what you think it does, so does it really matter why that is the case?"

"I guess not," I said, letting go of my dream of a scientific theory that would validate what I know about how story works. "But it feels important to explain why."

"But does it matter?" he asked rhetorically. "I guess that is the deeper question. The answer is 'probably not', because we know that it works. We know it works because of the emotional content in stories and that emotional content attaches to memory. In other words, we're just better able to remember things and probably pay more attention to them if they have a salient emotional content. Just tell people it works because it does."

I was willing to go with that. Marc shared one more important message crucial to being better storytellers and better listeners to other peoples' stories. We have a fallacy in our systems that he called the "Similar to Me" bias. We think that what is true for us is true for everyone. That's just not the case. We think it is, but in fact, luckily, we are each having a unique and fascinating experience and they often do not overlap. So, try to bridge the gap and don't imagine people feel like you do, or even see the world you see. This makes listening and telling stories all the more important.

Luminous Detail

One of the ways we can bridge that gap is the use of detail, visual imagery especially, but sensory detail in general. The poet Ann Waldman calls it the use of "luminous detail" when she teaches. Luminous detail apparently has some scientific backing.

According to Marc Hurwitz, "About 50% of the neurons in your brain are associated with visual processing in some way, which suggests, and it's probably true, that the more visual, the more imagery, the more evocative in that sense you can make a story, the better. Certainly, I would strongly suspect that given that half the neurons in your brain are involved in visual processing, the more visual imagery you can include, the more likely your story will be remembered and acted upon."

How To: Visuals Engage the Brain

Use visual details and other sensory details in our story. Describe everything. We are voracious in our desire for details. Help us smell and feel and hear and see what you are saying. Even give us pictures, snippets of song, or a taste of the cake you made – all with your words. Now, take this under careful consideration. There is such a thing as too much, and you know it when you read it. I remember reading many a Victorian novel in university and wondering if anything was ever going to happen, or if we were just going to have every blade of grass explained to us down to the dew point, when the dew lifted, the variegated colors one can expect, and you get the point. Try to keep it to the details that bring it to life, not kill it.

I heard about visual storytelling from many of the people with whom I spoke. It makes sense, our brains latch onto it and it sticks with us. Rachel Goble runs The Freedom Story, an NGO working to stop child trafficking in Thailand. Rachel came to the Freedom Story by way of a visual story, a film being made on child sex trafficking. Over the years of working on the issue, Rachel started to realize that while the stories told were riveting, and often lead to donors giving money to the cause, they were often biased in a way Rachel felt was unethical. "I realized a lot of small nonprofit organizations were struggling with needing to get louder to be heard and to do that, they created stories that generated pity. Those stories further reinforced stigmas rather than introducing nuance to an issue."

Rachel does things in the world; she's that person who says this needs to happen: a meeting, a conversation, an entire non-profit, and then she makes it real. So when she saw that there needed to be a place where non-profit storytellers could learn from each other how to tell stories in a better way, she created one called Ethical Storytelling.

She thought about what constructs needed to be broken down in order to tell better stories. Her goal, and the goal she suggests to other ethical storytellers, is to maintain the dignity of the people whose stories get told, to engage them in deep consent about sharing their stories, and to make sure that what they saw in their stories was a version of themselves that was beautiful, inspiring, uplifting, and resilient.

As an example, Rachel used a visual storytelling story to make her point. "Photography is tricky because it's such a singular image. A photographer who works in this space of ethical storytelling told me a story. She was working in Swaziland with a water organization and they were down by some really murky, dirty creek, and a bunch of people were coming down to that creek with buckets and getting water. She was on a team with donors to the water organization, and these donors all flocked to take pictures of the people collecting this dirty water because what they thought they saw proved their point about the importance of wells and clean water. So, before she snapped the picture, this photographer went up to one of the men and asked, "Hey, what are you going to use this water for?" And he responded, "Oh, just, um, you know, water my garden." So she asked, "Are you gonna drink that water?" He said, "No, of course not."

In all of her wisdom, she stopped to ask the question and not just use his image. That guy almost became the face of the clean water crisis when really, he was just gathering water for his garden."

Rachel and I laugh at this, but it's so common that it's a painful laughter.

"With photography, how often does that happen right? It can be so taken out of context. We need to be aware of the power of a single image."

I asked Rachel to share what we can to do to use visuals as ethical and powerful stories. She gave a list of tips that are the next how to.

How To: Using an Image

- When you take the picture, think about things like how the person looks. Do they look the way they want to look or the way you want them to look to make your point?
- Beware of your camera angle and how you catch the images. Angling the camera up makes someone look powerful, and down, pitiful.
- Think about wanting them to find something in themselves, when they look at the picture, that makes them proud.
- Create a caption or narrative around the image that puts it in context.
- In other words, tell their story the way they want it told.

Rachel herself is a powerful photographer and some of the best pictures of my family are pictures Rachel took for fun at one time or another. What makes the images stand out is that the humanity of the people in them shines out of the image and connects with the viewer in ways that highlight the spirit of the subject. I've seen my daughter showing pictures Rachel took of her to other people with a look of pride and awe. That is what we are going for when we reflect people back to themselves in story.

Stories on the Plate

I have had meals that were also stories. Food is such a great transmitter of culture and emotion that I'm tempted to use some neuroscience words about how taste and smell work in our brains, but I have given that up, so I asked Selassie Atadika. Selassie is a chef in Ghana, but she is more than just a chef or an educator, she uses food to tell cultural stories that create resilient communities. Selassie tells me a story by way of explaining what resilience looks like through food. "For this Coronavirus, everyone in Ghana is going out and buying Vitamin C tablets. We import the vitamins and if you're someone of a lower income, you're actually trying to find the money to go buy this imported Vitamin C. But, we have baobab powder and it's cheap. It takes three tablespoons of baobab powder to equal one dose of Vitamin C. You can get it in the local market, mix it with water and a little bit of honey and make a juice out of it. And you're totally sorted." However, people don't know, and so if you don't tell them the story of this plant, its history and how good it is, then the cultural connection is lost, as is the possibility of supplying Vitamin C locally.

Selassie knows more about resilience and disasters than any other chef I have heard of, because she came to the food world after working for the United Nations for a decade and not seeing the changes she wanted to see in disaster resilience. Now, she uses pretty food, some might call it fancy food, to let the plates do the talking. Her plates tell the history and food ways of Ghana, they tell about resource allocation and nutrition and culture and community. In fact, her ideal food story is where community, culture and cuisine are intersecting with environment, sustainability and economy. That's thoughtful food. "Stories are what allow me to construct and also, at the same time, deconstruct what I've learned. We don't have a lot of written history in Ghana, so what I know comes from my childhood, and my grandmother and Auntie's childhood stories." Selassie uses the stories to understand why her community eats what they eat, and then she uses it to tell a story of possibility, health, community, and change when she puts it on a plate.

How To: Stories on the Plate

We have all seen a million too many Instagramed meals. Let's not do that. You can use the food itself to tell a story of culture or aspiration, of love, family, history, and freedom. Try cooking a meal that tells your story. If you can, feed someone. If you can't, share the recipe and the story.

Possibility

Last night I was on a call with clients in China who I last saw in person in September. We were having a session on resilience and I was supposed to be providing them with skills and tools. That tool sharing did happen, but they were the ones providing us, in the United States and Europe, on the call with hope. "In Beijing we are back in the office," my sweet colleague in China said. "We are together again." I could hear the smile in her voice. These are the same people who brought us a cake when we came to work together in person, who put up balloons that spelled W-E-L-C-O-M-E on the wall. I could feel their generosity and care across the Internet. The sound of their voices, in the room together, cutting each other off to speak to us, it was a different world than the one I was in, in my home office, late at night, on week three of being at home. After the call, she sent us a thank you note, and with it was a picture of the team, in the office, all wearing masks, but back at the desks we saw in September. Each and every one of them had twinkling eyes above the masks. That picture is sitting on my desk now, as I write. I see hope, compassion, resilience, and community in the faces that peer out at me. I can learn from that picture how to be in crisis and know there is another side.

Lisa Woolfork said this a different way when I asked her about her blogging and her Instagram live moments when she shares stories about her experience; she said it triggers in people a sense of inclusion and possibility. "My experience is not unique. It is repeatable. This thing that happened to me, happens to other people. And, in this context, it shows up, and then it makes you feel less isolated, and like you can do something about it. Then you are not so alone."

Carmen Cool reassured me that this is all about connection, not performance, and not to sweat it. "I think in any story there's a connection to our shared humanity. So, if we can get away from these ideas of performance or what we think a storyteller looks like or sounds like, we can connect with each other in our shared humanity. Especially right now when it's so obvious how strong our shared humanity is."

Beth Slazak is the Manager for Education and Events at the Creative Education Foundation and an improv and humor teacher, as well as a beautiful vision on the computer screen with her cheerful pink sweater and her big, wide eyes.

Beth uses improv to help people feel that the places they have been broken open are also the places where there is movement and action. "It's just important for us to understand that everybody, everybody in the room, everybody everywhere, has gone through hell. If you get to the age of 21 and your life has been perfect, that's awesome. If you get to 50 and tell me your life is perfect, I don't believe you."

"In my own life, the worst possible thing that could happen

to me, happened. My husband came home and told me he was leaving me for another woman.

"It's not what tribulation you've gone through and survived, it's how you've chosen to glue those pieces back together afterwards. Some of the worst things lead to some of the most beautiful. The way we chose to help people see that was with the 'Because of that … ' exercise."

How To: **Because of That**

Pick your tribulation. What was the thing that has happened to you that brought you the lowest? Then tell yourself the story of what happened because of that tribulation by saying the tribulation aloud and then adding, "Because of that … Because of that … " until you get to a story that gives you hope. Here is her example: "My husband left me with three kids to support and no useful education with which to do it. Because of that I had to go back to school, and found the Creative Studies program I perused. Because of that, I took a class where I met my now dear friend Izzy. Because of that, she made me go to present at my first Mind Camp creativity conference. Because of that, I was able to do that session on resilience and improv. Because of that, I get to speak to you today. And these are great things that have happened out of something that knocked me to my knees, and if I'm willing to stick with it, I can find the awesome at the end."

Lisa Woolfork describes that by starting her own community, based on storytelling, listening and sewing, "I built what I needed. I built what I needed to heal from the harm of white supremacy."

Lisa Woolfork talks about "capaciousness", and it sounds to me like the world we create when we use storytelling. "It's a certain type of physical and emotional space. It allows for a certain form of a practice of redemption because it lets people have room to breathe. Unless you have room to revise, to stretch out and expand, you don't have room to make mistakes and discover new ways of being and to try things on. You get to stretch out your heart space. Capaciousness suggests the vastness of the human imagination and of human possibilities. It's an actual field of experimentation that allows certain thought experiments, certain ideas, certain practices to exist in a way that's not so punitive, where you get more than one chance to get this right."

Long Story Short

In this chapter there are techniques you can put to use right away. To go back to them, just look for the heading *How To:* and then the title. Sometimes you want a novel, the long winding journey, and sometimes you just want the *How To:* and that's this list.

There are also people mentioned who you might want to know more about. At the end of the book there is a Resources section where you can find all the people I interviewed and how to get more information about them.

How To: Point of View
How To: Create Empathy
How To: Listening
How To: Work With Your Brain
How To: Visuals Engage the Brain
How To: Using an image
How To: Stories on the Plate
How To: Because of That

Chapter 3

Everyday Heroes and Superheroes

Reginald Hubbard is not my idea of a Washington D.C. inside the beltway political operative. He says, "For starters, I'm 45 years old. I'm the first in my family to go to college. I'm a six-foot-two, Ivy League educated, Black male, in a society that demonizes and destroys us. So over the first 40 years of my life I just had this persona that I would get into, just like, we just attack, you know, if it's me versus you, and all of those things." Then Reggie discovered yoga and the teachings of Yoga philosophy. "I turned 40, so I'm about five years into this study, but in college I majored in philosophy and had a long life before, so didn't come to the practice of yoga and philosophy as a newbie. When I started diving deeper into the philosophical aspects of the practice, I realized that everything I just described to you about myself is a story rooted in the past and is not the present. To some extent, that story limits what's possible because I'm tethered to what happened in the past, which is no longer the only truth."

I met Reggie the day after a hero of both of ours, Elijah Cummings, Civil Rights activist and Congressional Representative from Reggie's home state of Maryland, died in 2019. Reggie had his mala beads on, he was wearing a political t-shirt and sweat pants and had that yoga glow going on. The speaker, Dr. Douglas Brooks, who you will meet later in the chapter, brought up the departed Congressman. "Heroes like Elijah Cummings not only embody and reinvent our democracy, but they stand for a possibility unrealized. They are the only serious representation of hope there is." He went on to say that our American experiment in democracy may have fallen down on the promises that we stand for, but that we are a country of heroes who define and re-define what it means to be free, brave, and generous. People like Elijah Cummings represent the best of who we are, and that their lives are constantly re-defining the possible for us as a country." This turned out to be poignant when I figured out Reggie already was a hero in that story. I thought he looked familiar, but could not place him. At the break, when I asked if we knew each other, he said, "You've seen me on YouTube." His eyes looked down but his smile peeked out from the genuine humility. "I was standing next to Rashida Talib when she said her famous 'impeach the @#$%&' line and then handed me the microphone." As the Congressional Liaison and Washington DC Strategist for MoveOn.org, Reggie was the convener of that party, and as he said, "When I brought that powerful group of women together, I should have expected something memorable to happen."

Radical Acceptance of the Present Moment

Reggie's view of activism is informed by story. "Telling your story frees up opportunities to notice the nuance and what happened before and what's happening in the present moment. Activism is being radically present and serving the moment as it unfolds before you. You become more capable of handling the present moment and then you have the freedom to choose what happens next, what possibilities you see."

How To: Radical Acceptance of the Present Moment

The first part of the story equation is: What's Going On. This is the description of the situation before we took action, before there was any kind of activism, intervention, change, growth or learning. Describing What's Going On starts us off on a heroic journey. Then, when we get to What Happened, we are set up for understanding the trouble and the change. Reggie Hubbard calls this skill "Radical Acceptance of the Present Moment". When you tell stories or listen to stories, pay very close attention to the details of the world in which the story happens, and to the actual thing that happened. In telling Reggie's story, he himself paid attention to who he was – the tall Black guy with the Ivy League education who studied philosophy, but still had some anger and a sense of combativeness with the world. That Reggie is the one we identify with. We can tell from that description who he is, and we know there is going to be some trouble. Be really good at the present moment through detail, through description, and through feeling. This anchors us in the present and gets us ready for what is coming next.

What possibilities we see in the future depend on the story we can tell about what happens next. Reggie says, "I'm blessed in that my grandparents told me a lot of their stories. I grew up in the context of their wisdom. Part of the reason that I went to Yale undergrad was from a story my grandfather told me. He said that when he was younger, someone told him, there's no way a *Nigger* could be that smart. He told this to me at fourteen, and for me, the fourteen-year-old grandson who liked listening to Public Enemy, I was like, What? So I had that as my grounding. That anchored me so that when the storms came, I had my anchor. I was able to go back to what my family taught me and succeed." That was Reggie moving into What Happened. What Happened was he met trouble like a hero. He linked his family stories to his present moment and then made a future.

Those Who Can Foretell The Future Are Best Prepared To Handle The Present

This idea of the past linking to the present and on to the future was echoed in a conversation I had with Ismet Mamoun. Ismet facilitates creativity and innovation, turning theory into practice. She noticed that her scientifically and technically trained clients were lacking in the capacities that could help them make a bigger impact: emotional intelligence, creativity, and storytelling.

Never one to go easy on a problem, Ismet decided to teach those skills to future scientists before they got into the work world.

This year, she was about to start her first class with students at a major public university. Then, there was no class. COVID-19 hit and the students were scrambling, the faculty were lost, and there was a sense of ambiguity and upheaval. Ambiguity, complexity, a lot of unknowns create a situation where creativity skills come in handy, so Ismet leapt in, throwing out her initial plans and leading the students in storytelling exercises. She asked the students to go beyond the Story Equation and tell her what they were going to do next.

"They came back to me saying it gave them such clarity as to what they had control over and what they did not. They knew what steps to take and what they were just going to accept. It was empowering."

She texted me and said, "I need to read you some of these for your book."

One student wrote about the sense of possibility when they saw that an abusive childhood was not their fault, and that it was over, and in knowing those two things they were free to choose something different. She read about a student who planned to change the lives of their siblings and cousins by living as an example of what is possible, and that success can still include fun. The students were no longer scared and alone, they were powerful and brilliant in their character and their possibility.

Ismet said, "Stories are so powerful because when we tell our stories, it forces us to reflect, to make the connections from our past to our present and because of that connection, the present is connected to the future, and we can take some control. It gives you a sense that you can do something. It brings clarity about what driving force you are going to put behind your life."

How To: **What Are You Going to Do Next?**
Answer that question and add it to your story equation, see if you can see the glimmer of the future you can create, and write it down. You now have What's Going On + What I Did About It +

What Happened = Story + What am I going to do next?

There is a truth to the stories from the past and how they inform us in the present and may help us shape the future. Our families and our ancestors pass on to us their histories and wisdom. We also gain their experience through our bodies. We have what research calls epigenetic trauma, which researchers believe is passed on through turning on gene expression in our bodies, and intergenerational trauma, in which what our ancestors experienced informs who we are and how we respond to things. So much has been written about the darker side of this intergenerational and epigenetic trauma, but there are glimmers of hope in the research, too, where we see Post Traumatic Growth and the development of skills necessary to survive and thrive. We have a built-in set of skills and tools that we have learned to face into difficulty, and we have been prepared.

Who better to have with you in an emergency than someone with generations of knowledge and practice in dealing with violence, oppression or difficulty? In the case of the families of Jewish survivors of the Holocaust, researchers found a high degree of self-efficacy associated with those familial experiences. There is also research that shows the "never again" mindset is one that can galvanize change in the world.

Story makes all the difference because it assists in Post Traumatic Growth. Dr. Daniel Siegel, who works with parent-child attachment and interpersonal neurobiology, says very clearly in his research, books and talks that parents who have had a traumatic childhood are less likely to pass on their issues to their children if they are able to work out what happened to them as children in a story. This is not a story they necessarily tell their children, but one they tell themselves. Once they have been able to make the connection between their childhoods and adaptive aspects of who they are now, they are able to be more attached and stable parents. Story quite concretely saves our lives and the lives of our families and communities. This brings us back to the "Because of that ... " exercise in the last chapter and reminds us that we have the power of story to tap into when we need to create strength and resilience.

Kelly Diels, a writer and a feminist marketing genius, looked at me so intensely that I could see the pupils of her eyes dilate when she began to talk about the survival skill she had from her family and her own history. "Telling the truth about your life is one of the ways you heal trauma, because trauma festers in us if we can't allow it to leave. I know that when I told the truth about my life, I was enlightened. I'm able then to look at the thing that's harming me, my pain and my response, whether it's a maladaptive response or a positive response, and actually do something deliberate about it. I tell people to remember all the traumas that you've come through, all the things that you've survived, because what that means is you already have the skills to handle this thing that's happening right here and right now. I am constantly reminding people: Remember who you are. Remember all the things that you've gone through, and you've survived, because you're scrappy and ingenious and did things to channel those traumas. In a bigger way, remember who you come from."

Story as Comfortable Distance

We are living, right now, in a time of crisis, and even trauma, in which we have the opportunity to encourage heroism in ourselves and the people around us. Beth Slazak, the improv teacher, reminded me of a musical that was made about Gander, a Newfoundland town that had to respond to the 38 planes that were forced to land there and the almost 7,000 people stranded there because of 9/11. The show, *Come From Away*, is based on the real experience of a tiny village coping with that extraordinary moment. That musical helps me remember what to do in this crisis when I get lost: care for the people around me, care for the people in need, and do the next right thing right.

How To: Music as Story

Find the song or musical or album that makes you feel the way you want to feel right now. How that feels is up to you. Notice what the feelings are, though, and what story they tell you about where you are. Share it with a few people and see what resonates. Ask them to share their musical story with you.

Fables

Reggie Hubbard used a biblical analogy to describe our current situation. "We have got to basically tap into a communal strength right now. When Joshua was circling Jericho, the people came together and their collective scream brought down the walls. Look at this time we are in like the seven days in silence that came before the marching in that story. Let's create the connection and create the opportunities for people to heal and grieve because on the seventh day, when someone says: 'Scream!' we got to be like, 'Get these people out of here!' Because if we don't do that, and people feel deflated, and people feel like 'Oh, this will never change, Are you kidding me? This will never change,' then we are in trouble. Everything's changing by the moment. It's time. It's time. It's our time. We've been waiting for this."

That biblical analogy is another powerful form of story, one that leans on some of our shared cultural heritage. That heritage can be as big and inclusive or as particular and specific as we choose, and varies based on the stories and traditions we grew up with, but leaning into stories that tell us about our shared history is one way to move people. In fact, some conversations and some stories improve with distance.

We have talked a lot about emotion, the body, and the intense contact of telling the present moment. Sometimes, that's just too much: too much for the kind of conversation you want to have, too much for our systems in the moment, too much for the situation. Sometimes, we just don't want to be in the kitchen weeping while listening to a musical and chopping vegetables.

If so, we can lean into our shared cultural tropes of myth, fable, religious stories, wisdom traditions, and even a little pop culture.

Kelly Diels calls the stories she tells when she is teaching people about marketing and the world, *fables*. She says that she uses fables to create a story from which people can extract moral and ethical ideas. "I write fables, but there are no animals in them. But, let's pretend that element of fables isn't necessary. I start with a personal story, and then I extract a moral political lesson from it. People see how that lesson plays out in their own lives. So for me, that is classic human storytelling across cultures."

An unusual way to look at fables, one I explored with Rashunda Tramble of Stay Woke Tarot, is the use of tarot cards to trigger conversation and story. She is in her office in Switzerland, where she works, and the light is fading in the room, creating a sense of mystery. "The issue is that sometimes we get so caught up with the mundane stuff that we don't know the story is in there." Rashunda uses the cards to take people on a journey where they can leave the mundane world behind. "I'm just laying out the cards and that triggers the story. They say, 'Wait a second,' and then the story starts coming out. It's relief for the person because it it's almost like 'I'm not crazy.' It's a lot of relief." Rashunda says "Why and change have a dance." The story helps you find the why and dance with the change.

There's a subtle and powerful pull to allowing people to draw their own conclusions and in not trying to force them to see things your way. In a world where we increasingly feel we are shouting at each other or we end up in conversations where we feel as though everyone has to agree in the end or someone will go home angry, storytelling and fables or stories with a strong ethical Point of View helps us bridge those gaps and have those tough conversations. They help us talk when we don't want to cry or make someone else cry, or when the conversation is just too hard.

I deeply love my mother-in-law, and think she is one of the best human beings on the planet. There's also a lot we don't agree on politically, and a lot of space where we could fall into an argument if we momentarily forgot how much we adore each other. So, when we are talking about hard things, which is necessary when you're family, we use stories. She tells me family history from her enormous store of tales, and I eat it up. I tell her about my family traditions which are a world away, and about cookbooks and food. We use them to pass the love back and forth, and even to instruct a little, but without force or the desire to make the other person think our way.

How To: Fables

You have either told or been told a story with a strong ethical Point of View that almost begs you to come to a conclusion about how you live your life or how the world works. I think back to my grandfather's story about teeth not having rank. That was a fable, intended to bring us grandchildren into a world where we stood up to power, where we did what we thought was right, and where we took care of first things first. You have those stories in your life. They live in children's books about hungry caterpillars or little trains trying hard, or in the repeated family lore. You can find them everywhere – just look for a story that is more like a finger pointing at the moon, and follow that finger to the moral at the end. Use them when you find yourself in a tough conversation or when you need to speak out about injustice, unfairness, or you need to communicate across some of the enormous canyons that can divide us. They will help.

Double Down On Your Passion

Characters in a story need to have desires, needs, wants, hopes and dreams. Because we are connected to them through both empathy and concern, their desires feel real to us. Desire gets a bad rap in our pop-psychology thinking about equanimity.

We've all been given a bit of predigested and incorrect wisdom that wanting things is what makes us unhappy. This is just not true. Wanting things is what makes us get up in the morning, it's what makes us open the computer, it's what drives us in our work, relationships and pursuits. As Douglas Brooks, the brilliant professor of Religion and comparative philologist, Reggie and I were together to hear, likes to say, "Everything wants to make a living." What he means is, we want to survive and thrive. Not just we humans, everyone and everything wants to succeed in its way.

Douglas also says the same thing about COVID-19, "It just wants to make a living. The stories we tell ourselves about this virus are how we create meaning. The virus is just wanting to survive." In our world, some things are not interested in our Point of View at all, and other things are frankly out to get us. Those two categories are what we call the antagonist in the story. In this case, it's COVID-19 and systems that are not set up for our flourishing or even survival. Their intervention causes the trouble that we deeply want to overcome. There is no story without desire and there is no story without trouble.

How To: Desire

Sometimes a story can be as simple as a list or a scrapbook or a folder of pictures. Pull together a representation of your desires. Find pictures of what you love. Put a playlist together that makes your body want to dance. Make a list of the things in your life that get you out of bed in the morning. Find movies and books that when you read them, you deeply want something.

Tim Hurson, the creativity and thinking expert talks about a phenomenon called "Future Pull". Future Pull occurs when you can create a story of the future that is so compelling and powerful, that it pulls you towards it like a huge rubber band. This is Martin Luther King Jr.'s "I Have a Dream" speech. It gives us a vision of what the world could be that we are not now. This desire Dr. King had for freedom from oppression, for justice, humanity, and love, that is desire that brings us to our knees wanting to be of service to his vision.

Future Pull can work the other way around too. We can have futures we desperately need to avoid. When climate activist Greta Thunberg addressed the U.K. Parliament, she described a future we are heading toward that we need to avoid. "Around the year 2030, 10 years 252 days and 10 hours away from now, we will be in a position where we set off an irreversible chain reaction beyond human control, that will most likely lead to the end of our civilization as we know it. That is unless in that time, permanent and unprecedented changes in all aspects of society have taken place, including a reduction of CO_2 emissions by at least 50%." She finishes her speech by giving the parliament an idea of what is possible and why she is motivated to take action. "Sometimes we just simply have to find a way. The moment we decide to fulfill something, we can do anything ... We children are doing this to wake the adults up. We children are doing this for you to put your differences aside and start acting as you would in a crisis. We children are doing this because we want our hopes and dreams back." She so clearly draws a stark and harsh world where there are no hopes and dreams, and one in which we can have them back. Which world do we want to inhabit?

Tim tells me, "It's only once you can name things that you can begin to think about them. A lot of people are uncomfortable with the idea of metaphor of poetry, and of story, because it is not as concrete as they want it to be. And yet, that's where the truth lies. That's how you name things. That's what's so great about story: it gives people an opportunity to see for the first time a new idea through metaphor and expressed in a way that they're not used to. With story we can see the truths that really matter, and without which it's impossible to actually solve problems."

Imagination is necessary if we are going to build a world where empathy and care, connection and community allow us to flourish, all of us, together, and equally. The existing structures don't do that for us. Care, money, healthcare, access, education, freedom and flourishing are not evenly distributed, nor are trauma, tribulation, fear and oppression. Imagination and story will allow us to build new systems and structures that at this moment seem incomprehensible. I would even say that they are the only way we will get to a future that is substantively different from the present moment.

My sister-in-law is a travel writer, and last Sunday she had an article in the New York Times Travel section. Considering that we are all in our houses, not able to leave except to walk the dog and get groceries once a week, I almost threw the entire Travel Section into the recycling bin without looking, until I got a text reminding me her story was in there. I reluctantly opened the section and felt that tug in my heart that tells me I want something. I wanted everything, actually. Every place, every picture, every word. They made me want to be able to explore the world, see people and things I know nothing about, immerse myself in the food and the places that feel like freedom to me now. That feeling, while painful on week three inside my house, made me feel resolute in doing whatever had to be done to get through this crisis in a way that all those people and places would be okay, and that we would all be able to find each other again.

We are seeing, right now, through the COVID-19 crisis, fissures we did not know existed. Kelly Diels tells me that her Baby Boomer parents are radical and outraged. They are looking at the news and seeing people dying and they are furious about it, about the inequality that lets it happen and the systems that don't care for us. She says that they tell her, at this moment, anyone with a conscience can't tolerate what we see, and we need a path forward to doing something about it. They feel the desire to do something, and that desire is what will bring them through all the hard parts of the story. They are just trying to figure out what to do.

Figuring out what to do is something Kelly has thought about long and hard before this moment. "I always tell people to figure out what their thing is," she says. "What is your talent? What is your passion? What is the thing that you're great at? Double down on that, do that thing. If you're a painter, double down on painting and paint radical paintings that make us think differently about things. If you're a writer, write more stories that help us see the future. If you are a social worker, speak up, tell stories to the powers that be in your social working hierarchy. Whatever you're doing, do more of that and be more visible about it, talk about it."

How To: Double Down on Your Passion

You know so many things now. You know what your stories are, what your body tells you when you listen, you know what you can change or impact through story, and here is where you begin to see yourself as a hero in this journey. Think about what your superpowers are. If that feels a little over the top, think about what people tell you that you are good at, where they reach out to you because your skills and talents are strong. Think about what you love to do, what makes you happy.

Often we are so bad at figuring this out. We can say we love to paint, or we like to read, but we see it as a skill that has no real power. We have a tendency as humans to undervalue the skills we are good at while over-valuing those skills other people are good at. This is dangerous, because as heroes of our own stories, we have exactly the skills we are good at to work with, so we need to know how powerful they are. We are sufficient to the task, and we can make it happen, but we have to see our skills as the superpowers they are.

When I work with groups – corporate teams or non-profit organizations or religious institutions, I always do an exercise called "What is my superpower?" No one likes it at first, because they don't see themselves as people who could possibly have superpowers. So, to get over the hump, I have the groups generate the superpowers for each other either out loud or on paper. Once people see all the ways the people with whom they work every day see them as powerful, they can start to let go of the idea that the stuff they "just do" has no value because they are the ones doing it. Then, they can add to the list once they are in the flow of ideas.

How To: **What Are My Superpowers?**

You can do this virtually or in person, but pick someone you trust, who sees you a lot and knows what you are capable of, and about whom you feel the same way. Ask them to generate a list of the things they would come to you for, the things you do well, the things you are known for, and the things that they admire about you, the things you do for other people all the time. Do the same for them. Then, you can share your lists and see the reality. The things you dismiss about yourself are actually important superpowers. It may sound a little science fictiony to you, but you really do have these powers with which you can change the world.

Stories From The Emerging Future

Science fiction comes up a lot these days. We feel like we are living in a world from a science fiction book or movie, and mostly when I hear people say "This feels like science fiction," it's not meant as a positive thing about the current times. What if it is a positive thing? Science fiction can teach us how to make new worlds and create worlds where what we want – health, happiness, freedom, prosperity, love, community, systems that support us, where those things exist.

Science fiction theorist Tom Lombardo, who wrote a book called *Science Fiction: Evolutionary Mythology of the Future,* which kind of says it all, told me succinctly about why we look to science fiction. "The starting point to constructing a good future is to imagine it. Science fiction creates narratives of the future. People naturally resonate and identify with stories much more than with theories or visions of the future. We are storytellers. We live by the stories we tell ourselves. In reading science fiction we become immersed in dramatic narratives of the future, which have a powerful psychological impact on us."

New worlds are built bit by bit, through the imaginations of people who can see a glimmer of the future. Sometimes the worlds are grim, filled with disease or oppression, fear or violence, but sometimes the worlds we find in our imaginations fulfill us and create capaciousness.

Tom goes on, "Science fiction both warns and inspires. It considers both dark and bright futures, for both perspectives are necessary in order to intelligently and passionately move forward. Since it warns and inspires, it provokes us into action, invention, and the act of creation.

Science fiction creates an immense mind-space of possibilities, both good and bad, and motivates us to pursue positive possibilities and work against negative ones."

Many of us, and I may be outing myself as a geek here, have a favorite future world where things look more like our hearts tell us they should. It could be the world of *Star Trek: Next Generation* or of *A Wrinkle in Time* or of *The Black Panther* or of the comic book heroine America Chavez in the Marvel *Young Avengers* Series. It could be M.K Jemison or Octavia Butler or Becky Chambers who creates a world of possibility for you, but there is a future out there for us that is radically different than the one we have, and we can live in it for a bit to see what it feels like so that we can create that here and now.

Lisa Woolfork calls this "You gotta go there to know there," which is a line from Zora Neale Hurston's book *Their Eyes Were Watching God*. One of the characters comes back from her travels and says she learned you just don't know about other places till you've seen them. Then she says that line: "You gotta go there to know there." Woolfork calls this Body Epistemology, or what we know about things from our bodies and our minds going together into an experience. It also is a science fiction strategy where we let the story, which we now know impacts our bodies, take us someplace new so we can know new things.

"It's difficult to imagine a future," Woolfork says to me, leaning into the camera when she says it. "It's very difficult to just create something totally new, like a new system. How do we create something completely novel without relying on the materials that we already know are conventional?" Body Epistemology is part of her answer.

How To: Science Fiction Worldbuilding

Do a little research on science fiction books and movies that might tell you about our world right now. There are queer sci-fi blogs, afrofuturist anthologies, indigenous speculative fiction, space operas about intergalactic respect, and there are oldies but goodies that can tell us what it is like to be human in new ways. Find one you can read or watch right now, and explore that world, that point of view and the specific heroism of those characters. You will learn a lot about the worlds they build and the futures that are possible. Take a look at what the world is like, and decide if you want to live in that world or not. Someone quite consciously built that world, and you can do the same.

Holding the Tension of Character

This takes me back to Eiljah Cummings and what Douglas Brooks said about him. The various levels at which we can create futures are a tension we have to hold as we are building these new worlds for ourselves. We, as world builders, need to know three levels of reality all at once. It sounds complicated, but as world builders we do this all the time. Worlds come in three flavors, What Is, What Might Be and What Could Be. We call this the "Maybe Doctrine" when we build our worlds.

What Is is our radical acceptance of the present moment. We use that to create the present moment, accept it, and are aware of it while knowing it is not the entire story.

Then we have *What Might Be*. What might be is like Reggie Hubbard's response to his grandfather's story that you can't be smart if you are Black. This is a resounding "WHAT?" followed by an Ivy League education. This is where you see what is best in the system you have, and you work within it.

Finally, though, there is *What Could Be*. This is what happens when we can think outside the current system. If we looked closely, we might want something bigger, better, more powerful, more inclusive, more open to difference, and full of more flourishing for more people than what currently exists. Rich or thin or pretty or successful or perfect by the standards of our society, that's actually thinking small. It's letting the realities of our current world dictate the possibilities we are. This is where you live life as if the world were a much different place and in so doing, you bring the world with you. According to the Maybe Doctrine, you need to do all three as you build the world of the future.

Václav Havel, the former president of Czechoslovakia, lived in these three worlds through some difficult times. Douglas Brooks reminds me, "Vaclav Havel taught us that you live as if the principles and values you hold are true. While the world remains irrevocably broken and unlikely to fix itself, your character stands in a deeper truth because you're living as if that were true. We may never get there, to where your principles become the way of the world, but you live in a higher state of contingency or deeper conditionality anyhow. You live as if."

He restated the three levels of the Maybe Doctrine as this –

What Is is a state of *Candor*, where you are honest about the present moment.

What Might Be is *Compromise*, a relationship between you and the world that can get sort of stable but maybe not revolutionary.

What Could Be is *Character*, you become the character that embodies the best of you and the things you didn't even know were possible but are trying to make real.

How To: Surf the Maybe Doctrine

Can you define for yourself those levels of your personal story, try them on for size, take them out for a spin? If you were going to live as if, how would you fill in "As if WHAT?" Mine is that the world is a just place, ruled by love. What would yours be?

Our job as storytellers and listeners is to live the tension of all three levels of the Maybe Doctrine at once. That is what someone like Elijah Cummings did and why he is a hero. He was pragmatic about *What Is*, he lived in *What Might Be*, and he was able to show us *What Could Be*. That makes the hero of a story deeply powerful and turns them into someone we want to talk about for generations to come.

Long Story Short

In this chapter there are techniques you can put to use right away. To go back to them, just look for the heading *How To:* and then the title. Sometimes you want a novel, the long winding journey, and sometimes you just want the *How To:* and that's this list.

There are also people mentioned who you might want to know more about. At the end of the book there is a Resources section where you can find all the people I interviewed and how to get more information about them.

How To: Radical Acceptance of the Present Moment
How To: What Are You Going to Do Next?
How To: Music as Story
How To: Fables

How To: Desire
How To: Double Down on Your Passion
How To: What Are My Superpowers?
How To: Science Fiction Worldbuilding
How To: Surf the Maybe Doctrine

Chapter 4

Please Turn On The Light

As this COVID-19 crisis grips the world, we have become a community of people who want the same things – safety, health, love, calm, a cure, community, and connection. I have been in conversations with the hospital staff who you met in the first chapter, folks in healthcare in Asia and Europe, clients all over the world adjusting to the new not-so-normal, and with communities in need who are not getting the resources and aid to stay ahead of this virus. When I ask them to type into the chat box on the call what they want to give the world right now, the same words come up over and over: safety, courage, strength, security, health, love, peace, comfort, humor, care, a hug, groceries, toilet paper, a cure.

We make those lists together, on Zoom or Skype, so that we can visualize the future together in a new way. Last night, I made another one of these lists with clients in Thailand, Malaysia, Japan, and Australia, and we sat together with the list they created, feeling like the things we typed were real and possible. One of the people on the call wrote in the chat at the end, "Thank you, I have not felt this hopeful in a long time. Even though nothing changed, everything changed."

How To: List Story

Sometimes a story is just a list. We visited that in the *How To* on desire. Here your entire story is a list. Feelings you would like to have. Places you want to go when you can leave your house. Things you would like to tell yourself in the future. Ideas you have had while isolating. Trees you love. Kinds of birds you can see out your window. Create a list that is in itself a snippet of your story that changes things.

Turn on The Light

When I was a child, I had a babysitter who told me vampire stories. I loved them. I loved the fear they created in my body, the racing heart and the sharpness of my mind when I was petrified. I kept looking for those feelings when I watched movies, and would sneak disaster movies like *The Towering Inferno*. I even watched *The Exorcist* one night, alone in the basement. The feeling of being alive and riveted kept me coming back even though I could not sleep. My mother would say good night, turn off the light in my room, and walk out. What was a bright, cheerful, yellow room during the day became a landscape of potential disasters and horrible monsters as soon as that light went off. I would imagine just how many vampires could hide in my closet, and what would I do if a fire blocked me from the door to the hall, and I had to slide down the roof, into the lilac bush, swing down, and run through the back alley to the neighbors' house to call the fire department and save my family from the blaze. I stayed awake for hours every night alert, sharp, and ready to fight.

Because of my nighttime vigilance, I fell asleep in class, I fell asleep doing my homework, basically I could fall asleep anywhere the light was on, just not at night in my bed when the light was off. Finally, after months of this, one night I crept out of my bed, flung the closet door open, and pulled the cord to turn the light on. The room immediately glowed warm and I got back in bed. With the closet door open and the light on, I could sleep. I slept with the light on till I went away to college. I was safe when I could see the room around me, the boring laundry basket instead of a vampire, the electric sockets not sparking killer flames, no devil hiding under my bed. It was a comfort, but more than that, it was a protection against the terrors that I knew permeated the world.

Story is that light we turn on for ourselves. It's how we bring our deepest fears into our waking lives and meet up with them courageously. In this moment, when all of our fears for survival are heightened, when we are anxious because we just don't know what's next, and when we are probably not sleeping that well, we need the light turned on, so that we can see our way to the love, peace, security, trust, and care that we want for ourselves and each other.

Sheva Carr, CEO of Heart Ambassadors and co-director of HeartMath Healthcare who was facilitating the call in Chapter 1, explained why those lists of feelings and the light they shed are so deeply moving and so powerful. "From the HeartMath point of view, the most important story we tell from a resilience perspective is the story we tell ourselves about a situation. When we tell a story about a situation that drains our own energy, that compromises our resilience, heart intelligence can give us access to new narratives about challenging events that can boost our resilience."

Sheva is a force of nature. She's a big presence with bright red hair and an articulate, compassionate voice who has been working on how to access our heart intelligence for decades to bring this field of study from the Institute of Heartmath to the world of health care. This puts her on the front lines of supporting healthcare workers all over the world right now.

"I've trained hundreds of physicians in Colombia who are facing Covid-19. Physicians in Colombia are experiencing great alienation and stigma. A lot of them are not being paid because of the government shut down, but they're still expected to work. They don't have proper personal protective equipment and they're being evicted from their homes because their landlords are afraid of getting COVID-19 from them. Talk about challenges and adversity." She sighed softly and I could hear Gingee, her cat, rustle on the couch. She told me that when people are in fear mode, or stress and survival mode, what happens is their heart rhythms become incoherent and their higher cortical function shuts down – this is what we call fight or flight mode. They can't see the situation clearly, and they get myopic. "We are teaching Heart Math to physicians and nurses and this is a big aha! moment. They suddenly shift from rage and despair at risking their lives and being alienated and not having their own needs met, to feeling this compassion in their hearts for the level of care and fear people feel. It shifted from that feeling personal to the sense of meeting them in their humanity, where we're all afraid, and it started a process of problem solving and solution seeking."

"In other words, you gave them access to find other stories, more resilient versions of what is happening?"

"Right. That pivot from justified frustration and exasperation and fear, to compassion, saves them a lot of energy to keep their buoyancy and enlarges their capacity to respond and adapt in the face of the challenge. Long term, we have lots of data that shows how that then prevents health consequences, not to mention turnover and burnout and hopefully PTSD. The health care providers and law enforcement officers, for example, who don't burn out using up all their fuel in reactivity, that's really resilience."

When I asked Sheva how she defined that word resilience about which we have been hearing so much, she gave me the simple answer: "The capacity to prepare for, recover from, and adapt in the face of challenge, adversity or stress." Built into that definition of resilience is the idea of adaptation, of change, like the rubber ball vs. broken bowl metaphors. You adapt and because of adaptation, you grow, change, and flourish.

How To: Your Heart's Intelligence

The Quick Coherence® Technique Step One – Heart-Focused Breathing: Focus your attention on the area of the heart. Imagine your breath is flowing in and out of your heart or chest area, breathing a little slower and deeper than usual. Find an easy rhythm that's comfortable. Step Two – Activate a Positive Feeling: Make a sincere attempt to experience a regenerative feeling such as appreciation or care for someone or something in your life. Suggestion: Try to re-experience the feeling you have for someone you love, a pet, a special place, an accomplishment, etc., or focus on a sense of calm or ease. (The Quick Coherence® Technique was developed by HeartMath and is a registered trademark of HeartMath.) This practice, for me, gets my body to send the "it's all okay down here" message to my brain, in a way that allows me to have that mental space that Marc Hurwitz told me is available for all the things storytelling and listening demand of me. It turns the light on in my dark room of freak-out and lets me see the shape of the world around me. Then, I can take story out into the world with bravery and resilience.

Crucible of Transformation

According to Douglas Brooks, the religious studies scholar, storytelling is where the broken shards of the world meet up with the broken shards of our experience and the result becomes a gift. At times, that can feel daunting. Those broken shards are terrifying, inside and out. We feel like we don't have the gravitas or the message or the clarity to tell a story that big and messy. We can. We must. We both live in the world as it is: scary and dark and unresolved, and we are able to act "as if" to be the very light that shines out in the dark, that message from the future of how it could be. We can do all of that at the same time without needing to be perfect or have all the answers.

I was talking to Bhanu Kapil, a poet and writer who was teaching at the University of Cambridge, and she was telling me the origin story of her first book. In that book, *The Vertical Interrogation of Strangers*, she published a heart-breaking fragmentary set of conversations with South Asian women about their lives. The book had an odd start. Bhanu, who can be shy and reserved, needed a way to talk to boys in London when she was a teenager. "So, my best friend and I invented surveys and would stop attractive young men and pretend to be university psychology students. It was a ploy to talk to them. It worked and that stuck in my mind."

Bhanu's curiosity about who has permission to tell stores and who doesn't lasted and she began to see that without the ploy of the interview, women who looked like her were not comfortable being in the spotlight of a story. She took up her interviewer persona once again as an adult. "That was in my memory bank, so I spontaneously started asking questions of strangers in airports – women or girls who seemed to be from Indian or Pakistani or Bangladeshi backgrounds. One day, my family was stuck at the Air Turkmenistan counter at Heathrow terminal 4. We were all sitting there, bored and unhappy, and I took out a pen and a notebook and went up to the woman working at the ticket counter and asked her the question that became the center of the book: 'Who is responsible for the suffering of your mother?' The woman behind the counter with the Glaswegian accent started to cry. She told me her story and I wrote it down. I began to ask the other women in the waiting area. I began to ask women who looked like me wherever I saw them. Over two or three years, I accrued questions and they brought up profound emotion and sorrow because they were physical questions; we did not have the word somatic then, but they were questions you had to process with your body."

Bhanu put those women in the seat of storytellers and invited them to find their stories. She did it by being the character of the interviewer, someone she really might be, and also by embodying the character of the listener, who we all could be. In that role, she made storytellers out of women who had no idea those stories lived in them.

Knowing Bhanu's story, I tried applying it. When last I went to a High School reunion, which was a while ago, I was nervous and a little put off by having to have conversations with all these people who were basically strangers, except for the fact that I knew them 20 years ago and had mixed feelings about them even then. I was recently divorced, the mother of three elementary school aged kids, who provided most of my social stimulation. I was still the glasses-wearing, geeky, somewhat awkward person I'd been in high school. Though I was living my personal dream of being a writer and a college professor, teaching Ancient World Literature was not cocktail party conversation unless the other person found the comparative use of the dative and genitive cases in Latin and Sanskrit fascinating.

Bhanu and I decided to come up with some questions I could use to elicit stories from the people who I would see, and who might otherwise send me to hide in the bathroom all night. The questions we devised were simple: "What makes you happy in your life right now?" and "What do you miss most about the town we grew up in?" I did not bring a clipboard, though I thought about it.

As I moved around the party, trying to figure out who these parent-aged people were and what teenager I knew was lurking in them, I asked the questions. I found myself in a steady stream of real conversations, with people who seemed genuinely happy to talk to me. Best of all, I became the compassionate, interested person I wanted to be. I was living in what Could Be, and it felt great.

How To: **The Interviewer**

This can be you too. By asking a simple question or two, you can bring people to life, you can be a really empathic listener, and you can create the world you want to live in right now. Create your version of those two questions – and take it for a spin. Ask your neighbor over the fence. Ask your friends. Ask complete strangers. Bhanu gives you permission to create a make-believe institution for whom you are asking the questions, if that puts you at ease.

One of the things interviewing complete strangers and people who are not usually cast as the heroes in stories gives us is the realization that we, those of us who might not be thought of this way, we are the culture makers. The interview widens the circle of story by one order of magnitude. We are now a two-person story team. We just made a culture. Think about how powerful that is – two people and one story changes culture.

We Are The Culture Makers

While institutions do have power, and systems of oppression are real, and we do need to understand how and when things are broken and not working, we are still the people who tell, hear, and repeat the stories that make the culture in which we live. To learn more about this, I called Kelly Deils, who in her marketing and storytelling genius coined the phrase, "We are the culture makers." I asked her what she meant by that phrase.

"My idea when I say 'We are the culture makers,' is we have been conditioned to believe that the people who have power in our culture are the people who are occupying the C suite or Congress, who are disproportionately white men. We were trained to see that world as power, and they're the people making the world and making the decisions. People feel like we don't have power and therefore we're too small and powerless or ineffective to make any kind of difference. But this moment in time exactly shows us, the world can't function without us.

"I think about that, in particular as a woman and as a feminist. The uncompensated caregiving labor of women in offices when they make everything run smoothly because meetings are organized and coffee is made and the agendas created or at home where relationships are tended to, nothing functions without women's uncompensated caregiving. We can see that in this moment in time, in the midst of a pandemic, that that labor is how we are all upright. How are we surviving this moment, a massive form of collective action where we're all staying home? We have the power. We are the source of political power, we are the source of economic power, we are the source of communal and familial power. We are the culture makers.

"When I look at everything that's good in our world, if we have civil rights it is because people who have no power in the system made it that way: women of color and communities of color, gay folks, trans folks, fat folks. So everyone on the margins who's taught to believe that we don't have power, we're the ones who make the wheel go around in this culture. Let's relocate that knowledge. We are the culture, and we deserve to make society and institutions so that we can flourish."

That last point stuck with me. We are the culture makers and we can make society in our own image. At this moment, what we can see in the COVID-19 crisis and our response to it is that the culture will need to be remade. We have the opportunity to be the culture makers who do that through the stories we tell ourselves and the stories we tell and share. We can be both the scared kid in the dark, the person who turns on the light, and we can be the light itself that shows things for how they could be.

Community, Culture, Change

We need support to live in a different world than the one we see out the window right now. We need to look past the fear and be able to look into the emerging future. That is resilience.

The first skill to break down the deeply frightening and disempowering dominant story comes from being able to listen and think critically to the stories we hear. Isabel Foxen Duke is good at the breakdown and build-up of the stories that make the world. As a teacher, coach, and activist fighting fat phobia and diet culture, Isabel uses her training in sociology to deconstruct systems and cultures in order to create stories that make change possible.

"How do you get folks to notice the water that they're swimming in? How do you help people see the culture in which we live clearly and separately from themselves?"

She tells me we need to listen to each other's stories. It cures the thing that ails us. "It's called terminal uniqueness," she says and then explains that we need each other's stories to see the larger system in which we live because, until we hear our story repeated over and over, we think we are alone and the problem is us.

This COVID-19 crisis in which we are living may be with us for a long time. It leaves us isolated physically and emotionally. Story is how we begin to bounce back. I turned to Meg Bradbury and her community, Elderqueer to understand more about community building through story. Meg hosts online gatherings for queer folks aged 40+ to connect and build community, with conversations about aging in body, mind, relevance, culture, and relationships.

"When I was starting to understand how my body was changing in terms of perimenopause and menopause, as a person with ovaries going through those changes, and could not find information out there that felt relevant to me. I put a call out and asked 'Who can come with me?' People answered and that ended up being Elderqueer. Everything we do is about the power of shared experiences. When you hear your experience told by another person in their own way, you connect to it because you find that you find the anchor, you find the similarities. Then, you also find in here the differences inherent to every individual's experience. You can marvel at that. That listening and telling are probably our most powerful cultural salve for what ails us."

Meg was so fluent and so comfortable in our online connection. I heard in her story both openness and vulnerability, those hard won but amazing story superpowers. They are unwieldy and hard to control and make most of us very scared. Meg's ease with them reminded me that community helps us get through the fear.

Story Leadership In Crisis

Reggie Hubbard said to me, "The two things we need to do as leaders are listen and be honest. We need to listen to people, find out where they are, and then, we've got to be honest with them about what's going on. In doing that, people learn to trust your instincts, and we need trust right now in this crisis because we're going to have to go through some hard things. If you're compassionate and honest on the top end, they'll be with you on the bottom."

I had the pleasure of speaking to two leaders from Hazon, which is the largest faith-based environmental organization in North America. Nigel Savage founded the organization and is the president and CEO. Hazon knows how to talk about disaster and how to bring people bad news, hard statistics, and frightening realities. Nigel shared with me a tool he uses for speaking to groups of any size, from small gatherings of ten people to rooms of 1000. "I always begin with the people in the room. If it's a small group, I'll ask everybody, 'Tell me a little bit about why you're here: something you're thinking, a question that you bring about the topic.' If it's a big room of people, I'll say 'Turn to your neighbor and share with them and then I want to hear from a few people.' We begin not only with stories, we begin with the other person's story. Only when I've heard even a little bit of their story can I then start to share our story."

How To: **The Other Person's Story**

Start with the other person's story. Before you share in a meeting, in a group, even one on one, start with the other person's story. Ask them what got them there, what they want out of the conversation, or how they are doing, and really listen. See if it informs what you are able to say and do next, because you understand them better.

I've seen Nigel in action. He really does ask people to share their stories. Then, after listening, Nigel speaks to the group about how the environmental movement struggles are because of this failure of story. "There are two things that have historically been part of the stories about social change in the world that have animated us. One of them is that we've seen something wrong and we could imagine success. The second is that we could imagine that somebody else was a bad person and that we were not. In relationship to apartheid we could say 'There should be a free democratic South Africa and wouldn't it be amazing if Nelson Mandela were president?' It's a very clear definition of success. And we could say, 'Oh, those people are racist. I'm not racist.' True or not, but we could certainly say it. With the environmental crisis, we can't define success. There is no likelihood that we're going to wake up to a headline that says "Great news, climate change fixed, go back to how you were." Secondly, there are no bad guys in climate change. We are all the bad guy. Fundamentally all of us have grown up in a world that is unsustainable and we're all part of it. We all drive or take taxis or get on airplanes or live in any number of ways that are unsustainable. So those meta stories underpin how we relate to the environmental crisis because we can't define success clearly and because we can't see ourselves as heroes of the story, it's hard for us to engage with the environmental challenge in the first place."

I asked him, "What do you do about it?" His answer was very similar to Reggie Hubbard, he said we need to call it out. Be honest. Honesty makes tackling an intransigent problem much more possible. "But of course, we're sitting here now and it's the Corona virus, which seemed to come out of a clear blue sky. It's a reminder to all of us that we're connected and we're vulnerable. That when you put seven billion people together in close quarters bad things are capable of happening. And that we can take individual action to make a difference."

What's At Stake

In order to tell the stories of change, we need to understand what is at stake if we continue the status quo and what is at stake if we change. Sometimes it's hard to see what is at stake if we change because of our biases towards the status quo. It is equally hard to see what about that status quo is so alluring. Becky O'Brian, Hazon's Director of Food and Climate has another way for individuals to take the enormous issues and fears around climate change and make them personal.

Becky begins to talk to people about how to change their thinking and behavior around food and climate by asking them, "What is your food identity?" She knows that this identity is deeply hard to shift and until we see it clearly, with some perspective, we don't understand our resistance to changing it.

Becky has participants in her conversations write or draw whatever answers they come up with on index cards and arrange them on a table anonymously. People write things that evoke their physical presence – describing their grandmother's chicken soup or their garden filled with leafy greens, or their culture, or their health, or family, or history. Then they put the cards on a table and look at them from a distance.

It's so hard to build a future if you are not willing to let those identities go. And, you can't let them go if you don't see them. Every hero, heroine, main character, and even the secondary characters in a story, go through transformation and change. The trouble and trepidation they face brings them challenges that change who they are. They lose their old identity and become someone different. In a story we see that as character development. In real life, those changes bring loss, grief, and even nostalgia for who we were.

In this COVID-19 crisis we are all different than we were when we started our new lives of isolation. In a meeting, I had a participant say to me, "Why is it that when I slow down at all, I am just so, so sad?" When she said that, I could see a screen full of nodding heads as everyone, in their Zoom boxes, agreed. We are being developed as characters, and it does not feel good. Under the scramble to adjust is grief.

Becky knows this from trying to help people see the nitty gritty of behavior change around environmental issues. It's hard to tell people "Eat less meat, don't fly on airplanes, stop driving so much," she tells me. Those are technical solutions that don't address the emotional battle of letting go of what you thought made you who you are. Story is what addresses the emotional battle. Becky ends our conversation by saying, "Sharing stories means you get to be someone else's happy ending."

How To: **What's At Stake**

Describing what is at stake if our stories work or fail can be a scary undertaking. But, it does galvanize us into action. I often use images to do this, like Becky and her cards. I will ask people to pick three images from the story cards I have. You can do this just from Google images. One image is who we are right now, what is our identity. The second is who we will be if we fail. The third is who we will be if we succeed. The story comes out of looking at those last two cards. The gap between them makes it possible to see the story of what's at stake.

What Is The Ceremony I Need?

The wisest person I know when it comes to calling forth the story in each of us, and in making the space and the place for honoring it, is Alexis Pauline Gumbs. She is a self-described queer Black troublemaker, Black feminist love evangelist, and aspirational cousin to all sentient beings. As my aspirational cousin, I asked her what her advice would be for all of us swimming around in the feelings of isolation, looking for a story that can heal and save us.

"The question I always ask myself is 'What is the ceremony that I need?' If I don't know what the ceremony I need is, then 'What's one component of the ceremony I need?' The ceremony that I've been in, while not leaving the house, is a photo album from the day of my christening. This is where I've been traveling. I've been traveling to this day where all these people, some of whom are still living, some of whom are no longer living, were all holding me.

"I like to time travel to this moment of being held by so many people, which is what I need now. Then I write about it. I didn't know if what I wrote would be shared, but I have sent out bits of it and it allows all the people who were present to time travel, too, to reflect on their lives from a different vantage point. The power of the story is in its specificity. It's so intimate, so specific to that time and our chosen family. If I tried to say 'What's the ceremony for all of us that will save the world and help us survived this virus?' That is really big. I saw the album and thought, oh, this is the gateway of specificity and opening.

"Opening is not simple in a time of a crisis, because it doesn't even really make any sense. On one level, people shut down, and sometimes you should close down and focus on protecting yourself. But, when I ask myself what would it take to open, because that's possible, I do believe that the ceremony can be found, without worrying about justifying how important your story is. This is not a grant application, this is about saving lives."

How To: **What is the Ceremony I Need?**

Alexis shared her snippets of story and photographs on Instagram, where I saw them, as did many of the people who were present at the time. She reported to me that the people who were there got to share in the feeling of community, closeness, and celebration that she evoked, and it felt like healing in a time of crisis. Alexis didn't set out to create story for the world, she set out to create peace for herself, and in so doing, she was able to bring people along for the change.

Create your own moment of ceremony using whatever you need to evoke a time and a place where you felt connected, brave, free, calm, all those feelings with which the healthcare workers began this chapter. What do you need to evoke those feelings? Give that to yourself and see if the specificity brings you a story.

Saving Lives

We all have stories that will save someone's life. Shanna Lewis, a journalist and radio producer who creates content for several media outlets told me how this works. "We all share some common desires, interests, and concerns because we all care about some of the same things – we all want to be safe and feel comfortable and we want to fulfill our basic needs and be in relationship with other people. There are certain stories that tap into fulfilling and connecting to those basic desires. They let us know how similar we are and so they speak to us. Then, there are going to be stories that we relate to emotionally and yet we have less in common with the storyteller, and we think, wow, I'm surprised I'm interested in this. For me that's sports stories. They hit the spirit of connection and love, but usually I don't care about the details. We realize through those stories that we are something like people we would not have guessed we had things in common with. Then there are stories that I am not going to connect with but they need to be told because someone else needs them, someone needs to hear those things, it's just not me today. When people worry that their story is not universal, remind them it does not need to be, it just needs to be their story, told with passion, because someone needs what they are offering today."

I was leading a call on the power of story and one of the participants told how one of her personal stories of openness and vulnerability hit her teenage son in just the way he needed. Her son was pining away for his girlfriend, talking on the phone three hours a night, and yet feeling separate. She told him her story of someone making her feel special. When she was much younger, her girlfriend wanted to make a gesture to welcome her back from a long trip. The girlfriend decided that the way to do this was to ride her bike 20 kilometers to her parents' house, where she was staying, and write the lyrics of a song they both loved on her parents' driveway. She came home to find the lyrics written out and the woman waiting for her. She said it made her feel so special and so loved. Her son thought about this and decided to create his own ceremony as a gift to his girlfriend. He took one of the moving speeches Romeo gives in *Romeo and Juliet*, and re-wrote it with his girlfriend's name. He recorded it and then sent it to her so that she could feel special, even in this time of separation. While I don't think a teenage boy would call it a story ceremony, his mom and I would. She took her story, which was pretty vulnerable if you have ever tried to tell teenagers sweet things from your past, and she offered it to him, not knowing how or if it would connect. Would it be the day that story turned on a light for him, or would it be one of those things where he made some polite noise and rolled his eyes?

In the end, you need to give your story up to the world, like our budding Romeo and his mom, and surrender in openness and vulnerability. This is what people who tell or share story do when they are done talking, It is what film makers, photographers, writers, and actors do when they are done with their work. It is what happens to every good story. Your voice stops. It's quiet. Then, there is that next moment. The story takes on a life of its own. It travels to the intended person and has an impact. You don't own it any more. The world does.

Isabel Foxen Duke has thought a lot about surrender, of giving up the illusion that you can control everything. "I think spiritual people really have an advantage because they're willing to flow with the tide. They see change as benevolent, rather than as a problem. You can move with the waves of where the energy or the environmental circumstance takes you, and choose to believe it's a fundamentally good thing. There are things you can change, and things you can't change. The biggest bang for your buck that can benefit your quality of life is the surrender piece, because it takes less effort and then you have room left to create new stories and new futures."

We begin by gathering stories that speak to us from inside ourselves and the world around us. We use what we know of the process of storytelling and listening to alchemize the stories. This changes the stories and it changes us. On the other side, we are different than when we went in, and the stories are too. We have gained and we have experienced loss. We have taken trouble and made it into character. The stories become the gift we give the world: the beauty that can grow out of what has wounded us, our brokenness, and the world shattering. That kind of gift has an impact. You can reach one person or a million people, it can be a phone call or a letter, or a recipe, or a driveway moment or a speech. They all take us to a similar place where we share our hearts and shed light in the darkness for the people we reach.

Much is at stake right now, and there is much to build and create. We save lives by connection, community, and capaciousness. It's a scary world out there, and we all have a lot to take on to create the world we want to live in on the other side. What you do matters, your story matters. Be brave, storytellers; you are saving lives.

Long Story Short

In this chapter there are techniques you can put to use right away. To go back to them, just look for the heading *How To:* and then the title. Sometimes you want a novel, the long winding journey, and sometimes you just want the *How To:* and that's this list.

There are also people mentioned who you might want to know more about. At the end of the book there is a Resources section where you can find all the people I interviewed and how to get more information about them.

How To: List Story
How To: Your Heart's Intelligence
How To: The Interviewer
How To: Status Quo Bias
How To: The Other Person's Story
How To: What's At Stake
How To: Radio Storytelling
How To: What is the Ceremony I Need?

About the Author

Michelle Auerbach is a geek who sees everything through the lens of story. She holds an MFA in prose writing from Naropa University and is completing her PhD with her dissertation on story as a technology for trauma aware change for individuals, organizations, and communities. She has published two novels, *Alice Modern* and *The Third Kind of Horse*, with two currently in the publication process. She writes for the *New York Times*, the *London Guardian,* as well as editing and ghost writing for several publishers and publications. Michelle is a former professor of Ancient World Languages and Literature as well as Creative Writing who brings the 6,000-year perspective on the possibilities that exist in our work life to show up as creative, engaged, strategic, and connected communicators. Currently she lectures in communication and story for changemakers and designers in the Environmental Studies Master's Program at the University of Colorado and at the Center for Media, Communications, and Information's Design Leadership program. She was trained in the 1990's by the New York City Department of Health, Kaiser Permanente, and through Columbia University School of Public Health on facilitation, group process, and individual and group coaching. Michelle uses storytelling and empathy as a way to connect Design Thinking and the creative process to team building and leadership development. Her clients include companies like Johnson& Johnson, McDonalds, and Mars, Incorporated, smaller companies who think big, and non-profits all over the world.

Previous Titles by Michelle Auerbach

The Third Kind of Horse
How does it feel to change the world?
In her new novel The Third Kind of Horse, award winning
author Michelle Auerbach answers that question and other,
more controversial ones, like what do lesbians do in bed, how
to make hash brownies, and how to get arrested.
It is 1987 in New York's East Village. AIDS is devastating the
intersecting worlds of drag queens, artists, and club kids.
Lyssa, a young lesbian, is working the phones at the AIDS
Hotline, trying to find herself, and some comfort, amidst the
chaos of the growing crisis. When she enters into a relationship
with Simone, the woman of her dreams, Lyssa finds the sexual
freedom she's been searching for, but her insecurities quickly
take over. Soon, Lyssa is in a complicated relationship with
Kevin, a recovering heroin addict, and her world implodes
against the backdrop of sexual politics and personal tragedy.
ISBN: 978-0-9569525-4-7

Alice Modern

Vienna is a city of tensions, fears, desires, and historic
momentum. It's the city of Sigmund Freud, the Viennese
Opera, the Jewish culture of the Austro-Hungarian Empire,
and portents of the future that everyone is striving to ignore.
Enter Alice Modern, who embodies a city spinning into history.
She is a Jewish girl living in a bourgeois household that, on its
surface, seems permanent and immutable. Alice no longer fits
into this static world, having served as a nanny for the poet
H.D. and her lover, the writer known as Bryher, in Switzerland,
and having been exposed to free love, promiscuity,
homosexuality, and women as artists and agents in their own
lives. This book is a tour through psychoanalysis, literary
history, and the ending of the old world through the loves and
passions of Alice Modern.
Modernist poet H.D. (Hilda Doolittle) and her lover, Winifred
Ellerman (known as Bryher), are central protagonists in this
story of 1930s Europe. In this graceful, erotically lush novella,
young Alice Modern tells the tale of leaving her bourgeois
Jewish home in Vienna to work as a nanny in the household
of H.D. and Winifred, caring for their young child Perdita.
Entranced by the keen literary lives of "Kat" and "Gryphon"
in Switzerland, Alice begins to transcend her tightly-bound life
and discover who she is and might become. Her world opens
and her sexuality awakens in a time of political turmoil and
existential hazard, reckoning with her own inner storms and
the approaching flames of fascism and holocaust.
ISBN:978-1-880977-44-6

Note to readers

Thank you for purchasing and reading *Resilience: The Life-Saving Skill of Story*. At this moment, you are in possession of a buoy or inner tube or a flashlight beam you can send out into our broken world. I want to continue to be part of what supports you in your story. We can stay connected, but the reach out is all on you. My website and Instagram information are below. Find me. Sign up for the newsletter. Follow me. I will keep telling you the stories that help me be brave and that re-make the world around me, and I will look for your stories too. You can also add a review of this book on your favorite online site, your blog, your podcast, your social media, or however you share stories. Please let me know you did so – my contact email is also below. It may take me 48 hours to get back to you, but I am listening.

Be Brave, Storytellers, you are saving lives.

www.michelleauerbach.com
@michelleauerbach on Instagram
contact@michelleauerbach.com

Resources

Ana Elisa Anselmo

Ana teaches her workshops at MindCamp in Chile, and can be
    contacted through their website.

www.mindcamp.cl

www.pensamientoproductivo.cl

Selassie Atadika

www.Midunu.com

www.midunuinstitute.org

Meg Bradbury

www.lamplight.space.com

@lamplight.space

Douglas Brooks

www.rajanaka.com

Meesha Brown

www.pcimedia.org

Sheva Carr

You can find information about HeartMath at

www.HeartMath.org

Information about the work Sheva does is at

www.pages.heartambassadors.com

Carmen Cool

www.carmencool.com

Kelly Deils

Writes a Sunday love letter you can sign up for on her website
    and teaches feminist marketing to culture makers.

www.kellydiels.com

@kelly.diels

Isabel Foxen Duke

www.isabelfoxenduke.com

@ isabelfoxenduke on Instagram

Cheryl Geoffrion

www.literallytheworld.com
www.linkedin.com/in/cherylgeoffrion
Rachel Goble
www.ethicalstorytelling.com
www.thefreedomstory.org
Alexis Pauline Gumbs
www.alexispauline.com
Hazon
Becky O'Brian and Nigel Slater
www.hazon.org
Reginald Hubbard
www.moveon.org
@oreggieglobal on Instagram
Tim Hurson
www.mindcamp.org
www.connect.mindcamp.com
Marc Hurwitz
www.flip.universtiy
Shanna Lewis
www.shannalewis.com
Tom Lombardo
www.centerforfutureconsciousness.com
Ismet Mamoun
www.mybeyonder.com
Jessica Pfeiffer
www.ntricateroots.com
Beth Slazak
www.creativeeducationfoundation.com
Rashunda Tramble, Stay Woke Tarot
You can sign up for readings, her blog, or read about tarot.
www.staywoketarot.com
@staywoketarot on Instagram
Lisa Woolfork
Lisa's podcast and Instagram feeds are full of sewing.

www.stitchpleasepodcast.com
@blackwomenstitch on Instagram

TRANSFORMATION

The *Resilience* Series

The Resilience Series is a collaborative effort by the authors of Changemakers Books in response to the 2020 coronavirus epidemic. Each concise volume offers expert advice and practical exercises for mastering specific skills and abilities. Our intention is that by strengthening your resilience, you can better survive and even thrive in a time of crisis.

Resilience: Adapt and Plan for the New Abnormal of the COVID-19 Coronavirus Pandemic
by Gleb Tsipursky

COVID-19 has demonstrated clearly that businesses, nonprofits, individuals, and governments are terrible at dealing effectively with large-scale disasters that take the form of slow-moving train-wrecks. Using cutting-edge research in cognitive neuroscience and behavioral economics on dangerous judgment errors (cognitive biases), this book first explains why we respond so poorly to slow-moving, high-impact, and long-term crises. Next, the book shares research-based strategies for how organizations and individuals can adapt effectively to the new abnormal of the COVID-19 pandemic and similar disasters. Finally, it shows how to develop an effective strategic plan and make the best major decisions in the context of the uncertainty and ambiguity brought about by COVID-19 and other slow-moving large-scale catastrophes. The author, a cognitive neuroscientist and behavioral economist and CEO of the consulting, coaching, and training firm Disaster Avoidance Experts, combines research-based strategies with real-life stories from his business and nonprofit clients as they adapt to the pandemic.

Resilience: Aging with Vision, Hope and Courage in a Time of Crisis
by John C. Robinson

This book is for those over 65 wrestling with fear, despair, insecurity, and loneliness in these frightening times. A blend of psychology, self-help, and spirituality, it's meant for all who hunger for facts, respect, compassion, and meaningful resources to light their path ahead. The 74-year-old author's goal is to move readers from fear and paralysis to growth and engagement: "Acknowledging the inspiring resilience and wisdom of our hard-won maturity, I invite you on a personal journey of transformation and renewal into a new consciousness and a new world."

Resilience: Connecting with Nature in a Time of Crisis
by Melanie Choukas-Bradley

Nature is one of the best medicines for difficult times. An intimate awareness of the natural world, even within the city, can calm anxieties and help create healthy perspectives. This book will inspire and guide you as you deal with the current crisis, or any personal or worldly distress. The author is a naturalist and certified forest therapy guide who leads nature and forest bathing walks for many organizations in Washington, DC and the American West. Learn from her the Japanese art of "forest bathing": how to tune in to the beauty and wonder around you with all your senses, even if your current sphere is a tree outside the window or a wild backyard. Discover how you can become a backyard naturalist, learning about the trees, wildflowers, birds and animals near your home. Nature immersion during stressful times can bring comfort and joy as well as opportunities for personal growth, expanded vision and transformation.

Resilience: Going Within in a Time of Crisis
by P.T. Mistlberger

During a time of crisis, we are presented with something of a fork in the road; we either look within and examine ourselves, or engage in distractions and go back to sleep. This book is intended to be a companion for men and women dedicated to their inner journey. Written by the author of seven books and founder of several personal growth communities and esoteric schools, each chapter offers different paths for exploring your spiritual frontier: advanced meditation techniques, shadow work, conscious relating, dream work, solo retreats, and more. In traversing these challenging times, let this book be your guide.

Resilience: Grow Stronger in a Time of Crisis
by Linda Ferguson

Many of us have wondered how we would respond in the midst of a crisis. You hope that difficult times could bring out the best in you. Some become stronger, more resilient and more innovative under pressure. You hope that you will too. But you are afraid that crisis may bring out your anxiety, your fears and your weakest communication. No one knows when the crisis will pass and things will get better. That's out of your hands. But *you* can get better. All it takes is an understanding of how human beings function at their best, the willpower to make small changes in perception and behavior, and a vision of a future that is better than today. In the pages of this book, you will learn to create the conditions that allow your best self to show up and make a difference – for you and for others.

Resilience: Handling Anxiety in a Time of Crisis
by George Hofmann

It's a challenging time for people who experience anxiety, and even people who usually don't experience it are finding their moods are getting the better of them. Anxiety hits hard and its symptoms are unmistakable, but sometimes in the rush and confusion of uncertainty we miss those symptoms until it's too late. When things seem to be coming undone, it's still possible to recognize the onset of anxiety and act to prevent the worst of it. The simple steps taught in this book can help you overcome the turmoil.

Resilience: The Life-Saving Skill of Story
by Michelle Auerbach

Storytelling covers every skill we need in a crisis. We need to share information about how to be safe, about how to live together, about what to do and not do. We need to talk about what is going on in ways that keep us from freaking out. We need to change our behavior as a human race to save each other and ourselves. We need to imagine a possible future different from the present and work on how to get there. And we need to do it all without falling apart. This book will help people in any field and any walk of life to become better storytellers and immediately unleash the power to teach, learn, change, soothe, and create community to activate ourselves and the people around us.

Resilience: Navigating Loss in a Time of Crisis
by Jules De Vitto

This book explores the many forms of loss that can happen in times of crisis. These losses can range from loss of business, financial security, routine, structure to the deeper losses of meaning, purpose or identity. The author draws on her background in transpersonal psychology, integrating spiritual insights and mindfulness practices to take the reader on a journey in which to help them navigate the stages of uncertainty that follow loss. The book provides several practical activities, guided visualization and meditations to cultivate greater resilience, courage and strength and also explores the potential to find greater meaning and purpose through times of crisis.

Resilience: Virtually Speaking
Communicating at a Distance
by Teresa Erickson and Tim Ward

To adapt to a world where you can't meet face-to-face – with air travel and conferences cancelled, teams working from home – leaders, experts, managers and professionals all need to master the skills of virtual communication. Written by the authors of *The Master Communicator's Handbook*, this book tells you how to create impact with your on-screen presence, use powerful language to motivate listening, and design compelling visuals. You will also learn techniques to prevent your audience from losing attention, to keep them engaged from start to finish, and to create a lasting impact.

Resilience: Virtual Teams
Holding the Center When You Can't Meet Face-to-Face
by Carlos Valdes-Dapena

In the face of the COVID-19 virus organizations large and small are shuttering offices and factories, requiring as much work as possible be done from people's homes. The book draws on the insights of the author's earlier book, *Lessons from Mars*, providing a set of the powerful tools and exercises developed within the

Mars Corporation to create high performance teams. These tools have been adapted for teams suddenly forced to work apart, in many cases for the first time. These simple secrets and tested techniques have been used by thousands of teams who know that creating a foundation of team identity and shared meaning makes them resilient, even in a time of crisis.